Terrorism

Other Books in the Issues on Trial Series:

Terrorism

David M. Haugen and Susan Musser, Book Editors

GREENHAVEN PRESS
A part of Gale, Cengage Learning

GALE
CENGAGE Learning

Detroit • New York • San Francisco • New Haven, Conn • Waterville, Maine • London

GALE
CENGAGE Learning

Christine Nasso, *Publisher*
Elizabeth Des Chenes, *Managing Editor*

For more information, contact:
Greenhaven Press
27500 Drake Rd.
Farmington Hills, MI 48331-3535
Or you can visit our Internet site at gale.cengage.com.

For product information and technology assistance, contact us at

Gale Customer Support, 1-800-877-4253
For permission to use material from this text or product, submit all requests online at www.cengage.com/permissions

Further permissions questions can be emailed to permissionrequest@cengage.com

Articles in Greenhaven Press anthologies are often edited for length to meet page requirements. In addition, original titles of these works are changed to clearly present the main thesis and to explicitly indicate the author's opinion. Every effort is made to ensure that Greenhaven Press accurately reflects the original intent of the authors. Every effort has been made to trace the owners of copyrighted material.

Cover photograph reproduced by permission of © Reuters/Akbar Baloch/Corbis.

LIBRARY OF CONGRESS CATALOGING-IN-PUBLICATION DATA

Terrorism / David M. Haugen and Susan Musser, book editors.
  p. cm. -- (Issues on trial)
 Includes bibliographical references and index.
 ISBN-13: 978-0-7377-3982-4 (hardcover)
 1. Terrorists--Legal status, laws, etc.--United States. 2. War on Terrorism, 2001---Law and legislation--United States. 3. Trials (Terrorism)--United States. 4. Detention of persons--United States. 5. Civil rights--United States. I. Haugen, David M., 1969- II. Musser, Susan.
 KF9430.T468 2008
 345.73'02--dc22

                                                          2008008897

Printed in the United States of America
2 3 4 5 6 7 12 11 10 09 08

 JUN   2009

Contents

Chapter 1: Trying Terrorist Suspects in U.S. Federal Courts

Chapter 2: Affirming Due Process Rights for U.S. Citizens Deemed Enemy Combatants

Chapter 3: Military Commissions Violate the Law

Chapter 4: Can Suspected Terrorists Be Held Indefinitely Without Charge?

Foreword

The U.S. courts have long served as a battleground for the most highly charged and contentious issues of the time. Divisive matters are often brought into the legal system by activists who feel strongly for their cause and demand an official resolution. Indeed, subjects that give rise to intense emotions or involve closely held religious or moral beliefs lay at the heart of the most polemical court rulings in history. One such case was *Brown v. Board of Education* (1954), which ended racial segregation in schools. Prior to *Brown*, the courts had held that blacks could be forced to use separate facilities as long as these facilities were equal to that of whites.

For years many groups had opposed segregation based on religious, moral, and legal grounds. Educators produced heartfelt testimony that segregated schooling greatly disadvantaged black children. They noted that in comparison to whites, blacks received a substandard education in deplorable conditions. Religious leaders such as Martin Luther King Jr. preached that the harsh treatment of blacks was immoral and unjust. Many involved in civil rights law, such as Thurgood Marshall, called for equal protection of all people under the law, as their study of the Constitution had indicated that segregation was illegal and un-American. Whatever their motivation for ending the practice, and despite the threats they received from segregationists, these ardent activists remained unwavering in their cause.

Those fighting against the integration of schools were mainly white southerners who did not believe that whites and blacks should intermingle. Blacks were subordinate to whites, they maintained, and society had to resist any attempt to break down strict color lines. Some white southerners charged that segregated schooling was *not* hindering blacks' education. For example, Virginia attorney general J. Lindsay Almond asserted, "With the help and the sympathy and the love and respect of the white people of the South, the colored man has risen under that educational process to a place of eminence and respect throughout the nation. It has served him well." So when the Supreme Court ruled against the segregationists in *Brown*, the South responded with vociferous cries of protest. Even government leaders criticized the decision. The governor of Arkansas, Orval Faubus, stated that he would not "be a party to any attempt to force acceptance of change to which the people are so overwhelmingly opposed." Indeed, resistance to integration was so great that when black students arrived at the formerly all-white Central High School in Arkansas, federal troops had to be dispatched to quell a threatening mob of protesters.

Nevertheless, the *Brown* decision was enforced and the South integrated its schools. In this instance, the Court, while not settling the issue to everyone's satisfaction, functioned as an instrument of progress by forcing a major social change. Historian David Halberstam observes that the *Brown* ruling "deprived segregationist practices of their moral legitimacy. . . . It was therefore perhaps the single most important moment of the decade, the moment that separated the old order from the new and helped create the tumultuous era just arriving." Considered one of the most important victories for civil rights, *Brown* paved the way for challenges to racial segregation in many areas, including on public buses and in restaurants.

In examining *Brown*, it becomes apparent that the courts play an influential role—and face an arduous challenge—in shaping the debate over emotionally charged social issues. Judges must balance competing interests, keeping in mind the high stakes and intense emotions on both sides. As exemplified by *Brown*, judicial decisions often upset the status quo and initiate significant changes in society. Greenhaven Press's Issues on Trial series captures the controversy surrounding influential court rulings and explores the social ramifications of such decisions from varying perspectives. Each anthology highlights one social issue—such as the death penalty, students' rights, or wartime civil liberties. Each volume then focuses on key historical and contemporary court cases that helped mold the issue as we know it today. The books include a compendium of primary sources—court rulings, dissents, and immediate reactions to the rulings—as well as secondary sources from experts in the field, people involved in the cases, legal analysts, and other commentators opining on the implications and legacy of the chosen cases. An annotated table of contents, an in-depth introduction, and prefaces that overview each case all provide context as readers delve into the topic at hand. To help students fully probe the subject, each volume contains book and periodical bibliographies, a comprehensive index, and a list of organizations to contact. With these features, the Issues on Trial series offers a well-rounded perspective on the courts' role in framing society's thorniest, most impassioned debates.

Introduction

On September 20, 2001, during an address to Congress and the American people, President George W. Bush recalled how nine days earlier the United States had experienced a devastating attack that forever altered the United States, its national security, its foreign relations, and its global agenda. The president asserted that on September 11 "enemies of freedom" carried out "an act of war" against America. Avoiding a description of the events of that fateful day when members of the Islamic extremist organization al Qaeda hijacked airliners and crashed them into the World Trade Center in New York and the Pentagon in Washington, D.C., President Bush enumerated the casualties of the tragedy and discussed the consequences, for America and the world, of such a brazen and deadly strike. He suggested that everything would change in the new age of terror, stating simply, "Night fell on a different world, a world where freedom itself is under attack."

Although terrorism is not a new phenomenon and is no stranger to American soil, the September 11 attacks were the most destructive and—with 2,998 victims—the most lethal. Indeed, the "different world" the president spoke of had much to do with the fact that the United States effectively had declared war on terrorism following the attacks. Unlike previous global wars, the Bush administration's ongoing war on terror is not about defeating a standing army but about securing airlines and ports, freezing terrorists' assets, monitoring terrorist cells, depriving terrorists of safe harbor, and interrogating captives who might know something about future plots. In part because it is an unusual war, the country has not uniformly rallied around the cause of defeating the enemy. Although no one wishes to see a follow-up to September 11, the ill-defined nature and the atypical conduct of the war on terror has divided public sentiment for and against the president's agenda. Many believe that defeating a shadowy terrorist group like al Qaeda demands decisive and unfettered executive action, but others are concerned that the White House is willing to sacrifice civil liberties and human rights in pursuit of counterterrorism.

Because of such concerns, the war on terror has witnessed an unprecedented clash between the executive and judicial branches of the federal government. Within the first six years of the war on terror, the U.S. Supreme Court has heard six cases arising from complaints against executive wartime powers. All of these cases have been waged by individuals captured during the early years of the war, and all question the right of the president to detain persons indefinitely without legal recourse to challenge their detention.

The Bush administration has steadfastly maintained in these instances that the Constitution invests the president with broad powers in times of war and that the Authorization to Use Military Force (AUMF), which Congress passed a week after the September 11 attacks, grants the president the power to use "all necessary and appropriate force" against anyone who "planned, authorized, committed or aided" the plot or harbored those who did. Such power, the administration has argued, includes the right to detain captives who pose a threat to national security. Furthermore, the administration claims that by act of a presidential military order issued in November 2001, the executive branch decreed that it could hold terrorist suspects indefinitely and try them for their alleged crimes before military commissions that operated outside the U.S. legal system. This order, the administration affirmed, strips the courts of the right to hear the petitions of detainees, and the separation of powers dictated by the Constitution further bars the courts from interfering in issues of national security.

The Supreme Court has not been easily swayed by these assertions of executive authority. Although the majority of justices who have heard these cases have agreed that the president has the power to detain enemy combatants under wartime prerogative, the Court has not been willing to concede that prisoners have no right to the writ of habeas corpus—the legal petition asking that a court decide if an individual is properly detained. The Court has also accepted some petitioners' claims that military commissions—at least as initially established—are not legally constituted venues appropriate for trying detainees because they lack some protections provided by the U.S. military code and international war conventions. Justice Sandra Day O'Connor, who gave the Court's ruling in one of the terrorism cases, *Hamdi v. Rumsfeld* (2004), went further by insisting that the judicial branch cannot be ignored in times of national emergency. Denying the administration's claim that the separation of powers mandated by the Constitution clearly circumscribes the courts, O'Connor asserted, "Whatever power the United States Constitution envisions for the Executive in its exchanges with other nations or with enemy organizations in times of conflict, it most assuredly envisions a role for all three branches when individual liberties are at stake."

Despite the involvement of the Supreme Court in these cases and its apparent rebuke of the Bush administration's assertions of power, many observers contend that the adverse rulings are minor obstacles to the executive will. In a 2007 article for *Slate* magazine, commentator Dahlia Lithwick went so far as to say that "the Bush administration keeps winning by losing." For instance, after petitioners questioned the legality of trial by military commissions in *Hamdan v. Rumsfeld* (2006), the president sought and gained congressional approval for the Military Commissions Act of 2006 (MCA), which declares military commissions to be legitimate and sanctioned venues for trying enemy combatants. The MCA also states plainly that "no court, justice, or judge shall have jurisdiction to hear or consider an application for a writ of habeas corpus filed by or on behalf of an alien detained by the United States who has been determined by the United States to have been properly detained as an enemy combatant or is awaiting such determination," effectively ending detainees' relief through the court system. However, in two related cases brought before the Supreme Court at the end of 2007, petitioners are questioning the legality of the MCA and whether Congress can legitimately enact legislation that would suspend the "Great Writ" of habeas corpus.

In addition to hearing the momentous concerns about the Great Writ, the federal court system has also been the setting of an equally controversial spectacle in the form of the trial of Zacarias Moussaoui, the first terrorist suspect arraigned before U.S. courts in connection with the September 11 attacks. The trial of Moussaoui had nothing to do with curbing presidential authority or interpreting Constitutional law, but it did raise concerns about whether Moussaoui was a scapegoat for the government's need to demonstrate to the American people that it could hold someone accountable for the tragedy.

From the outset of the five-year-long trial, which began in 2002, the defendant's sanity was in question as well as the government's (and even Moussaoui's) claims that he was part of the al Qaeda plot. The government's charge was based on testimony and documents that many commentators believed were circumstantial at best; even al Qaeda detainees dismissed Moussaoui's part in the plot, attesting that he was deluded and too unpredictable to trust with such a well-coordinated mission. Yet Moussaoui surprised the court in 2005 when he pled guilty to the six counts of conspiracy and told the jury that he was supposed to be the pilot of a plane intended to crash into the White House on the day of the attacks. At his sentencing trial the following year, Moussaoui stated that he wished the attacks of September 11 "could have gone on the 12th, the 13th, the 14th, the 15th, the 16th, the 17th." Still, many doubted his part in the plot and believed he was mostly bluster and bravado. Begging for the court's leniency, his defense lawyer, paraphrasing Shakespeare, referred to him as "sound and fury, accomplishing nothing." By one vote, the sentencing jury eschewed the death penalty and conferred on Moussaoui six life sentences.

In *Issues on Trial: Terrorism*, critics and commentators discuss the appropriateness of the Moussaoui verdict and sentencing as well as four of the U.S. Supreme Court rulings involving the war on terror. At issue in these court cases are not only the detention and punishment of terrorists but also the liberties that Americans cherish and the role of the judiciary in the government. Furthermore, the outcomes of these cases say much about the working principles of democracy and the values that America prizes. Speaking for the American Bar Association, Robert Hirshon maintains that the United States must bring to justice the terrorists responsible for the September 2001 tragedy, "but we need to do it in a way that respects core American values of due process and fundamental fairness—principles that have governed our justice system since its founding. To do any less would deprecate our Constitution and the memory of those who perished on and after the morning of Sept. 11." How the nation chooses to prove its commitment to justice in the war on terror will continue to be played out in the courts and will ultimately account for much of the price America is willing to pay for victory.

CHAPTER 1

Trying Terrorist Suspects in U.S. Federal Courts

Case Overview:
The United States of America v. Zacarias Moussaoui (2002)

On August 16, 2001, FBI agents arrested Zacarias Moussaoui in Eagan, Minnesota, on an immigration violation charge after a local flight school instructor provided information about a suspicious individual training on a Boeing 747 simulator. Apprehensive of Moussaoui's reasons for attending flight school, FBI agent Harry Samit and others attempted to obtain the proper clearances to investigate Moussaoui further but were unsuccessful in securing warrants allowing searches of his computer and personal residence.

Less than a month later, on September 11, 2001, nineteen members of the al Qaeda terrorist organization hijacked commercial jets, crashing two into the World Trade Center in New York and a third into the Pentagon in Washington, D.C. A fourth plane went down in rural Pennsylvania when passengers revolted, preventing the hijackers from reaching their target. Following the attacks, the FBI again turned to their French Moroccan detainee in Minnesota and received the needed permission to fully investigate Moussaoui and search his belongings. What the agents found tied Moussaoui not only to al Qaeda but also to the September 11 terrorist plot. The authorities went so far as to suggest Moussaoui was supposed to have been the twentieth hijacker on the ill-fated flights.

Based on evidence found through these searches in addition to information gained through interrogations of Moussaoui and other al Qaeda captives, an indictment of the would-be terrorist was issued by a federal grand jury on December 11, 2001. The U.S. government charged Moussaoui with six felony counts of conspiracy connecting him to the September 11 attacks.

Moussaoui's criminal trial began on January 2, 2002, and triggered nationwide debate over the proper trial and punishment of individuals conspiring to commit acts of terrorism against the United States. Some of this debate, however, was overshadowed by Moussaoui's erratic actions during the court proceedings. At various points during the nearly five-year-long court contest, Moussaoui refused to enter pleas on his charges, accused his court-appointed lawyers of working with the prosecution, and briefly took on the task of representing himself. Then, after pleading guilty to all charges against him on April 22, 2005, Moussaoui stated that his "conspiracy" was a plan to free Sheikh Omar Abdel-Rahman, the individual held responsible for the 1993 bombings of the World Trade Center, and had nothing to do with the September 11 attacks.

During the sentencing trial, the prosecution still attempted to prove that Moussaoui was directly connected with the September 11 plot and that he lied about pertinent details upon his initial arrest that would have enabled the government to prevent the ensuing tragedy. U.S. Attorney Robert Spencer argued that Moussaoui was a culprit either way and should receive the death penalty. Defense attorney Edward MacMahon countered that while Moussaoui was undoubtedly a terrorist who wished harm against the United States, his actions would not necessarily have resulted in the arrest of the al Qaeda hijackers prior to September 11 because he had no knowledge of specific plot details. MacMahon asserted that the death penalty would only incite others to follow Moussaoui into martyrdom for the al Qaeda cause.

On May 3, 2006, a federal jury sentenced Moussaoui to life in prison for his role in the September 11 attacks. In the aftermath of the trial, the conduct of nearly everyone involved and the final sentence have received both criticism and praise. To date, no other individual has been brought before a U.S. court in connection with these attacks, and it remains to be seen whether the courts will continue to be used for trying suspected terrorists or whether an alternate system such as military tribunals or international courts will become the preferred venue.

"Moussaoui's part in the end was to lie to allow his al Qaeda brothers to go forward with a plot to kill Americans."

Moussaoui Deserves Death for His Role in the 9/11 Terrorist Attacks

Robert Spencer

March 6, 2006, marked the commencement of the sentencing phase of the U.S. District Court trial of Zacarias Moussaoui, the man charged with being the "twentieth hijacker" in the September 11, 2001, al Qaeda terrorist attacks against America. During the course of the entire trial—which began in 2002—Moussaoui admitted to ties with al Qaeda and varying levels of involvement in the September 11 plot. Though no evidence has yet been put forth to prove Moussaoui's contribution to the attacks, U.S. attorney Robert Spencer argues in his opening statements at the sentencing hearing that Moussaoui had a role. Spencer claims that had the accused disclosed upon his initial arrest in August 2001 the information gleaned throughout the trial, the U.S. government would have taken measures to prevent the attacks entirely. Therefore, Spencer calls on the jury to hold the defendant accountable for lies told upon his original arrest, and he insists that in hiding the plot, Moussaoui actively participated in the attacks that killed nearly three thousand people.

Robert Spencer, "Opening Statement of the Prosecution," *United States v. Zacarias Moussaoui*, March 6, 2006.

September 11th, 2001 dawned clear, crisp and blue in the northeast United States. In lower Manhattan in the Twin Towers of the World Trade Center, workers sat down at their desks tending to e-mail and phone messages from the previous days.

In the Pentagon in Arlington, Virginia, military and civilian personnel sat in briefings, were focused on their paperwork.

In those clear blue skies over New York, over Virginia, and over Pennsylvania, in two American Airlines jets and in two United Airlines jets, weary travelers sipped their coffee and read their morning papers as flight attendants made their first rounds.

And in fire and police stations all over New York City, the bravest among us reported for work. It started as an utterly normal day, but a day that started so normally and with such promise, soon became a day of abject horror. By morning's end, 2,972 people were slaughtered in cold blood.

And that clear, blue sky became clouded with dark smoke that rose from the Trade Towers of New York, from the Pentagon in Virginia, and from a field in rural Pennsylvania. And within a few hours out of that clear, blue sky came terror, pain, misery, and death, and those 2,972 never again saw their loved ones, never again gave their kids a goodnight kiss. That day, September 11th, 2001, became a defining moment, not just for 2,972 families, but for a generation.

Killers were among us that day and for more than just that day. Those killers had lived among us for months, planned for years to cut our throats, hijack our planes, and crash them into buildings to burn us alive.

On that day, September 11, 2001, a group of cold-blooded killers from distant lands capped their plan, their conspiracy, to kill as many innocent Americans as possible. Those killers, part of the terrorist group al Qaeda, came up with their plan, trained for it, practiced it, worked on it, kept it secret, and then carried it out, hijacking four commercial planes on September 11 and crashing them on purpose to kill as many Americans as they could.

Moussaoui Enabled Attacks

One of the people in that plan, one of the conspirators is among us still, right here in this courtroom today. That man is the defendant, Zacarias Moussaoui. He is a loyal al Qaeda soldier, as were the other al Qaeda murderers. He trained to kill, as did the other murderers. He did his part, as did the other murderers, and he succeeded, as did the other murderers, including their leader, Usama Bin Laden.

Moussaoui's part in the end was to lie to allow his al Qaeda brothers to go forward with a plot to kill Americans. He lied so that the plot could proceed unimpeded, and that's exactly what he did. He lied and nearly 3,000 people perished. Moussaoui stands before you today, an admitted terrorist, a convicted terrorist, a proud and unrepentant terrorist. He pled guilty, as the Court has already told you, on April 22nd, 2005 to all charges against him in this case.

He is guilty. This trial is to decide what his punishment shall be.

On that day, September 11th, 2001, Moussaoui was a member of al Qaeda. On that day Moussaoui was part of the plot to hijack planes and crash them into U.S. buildings to kill as many U.S. Americans as possible. Moussaoui trained with al Qaeda as part of the plot. Moussaoui traveled to the U.S. as part of the plot. Moussaoui took flight training as part of the plot. Moussaoui purchased short-bladed knives, all part of the plot, all financed by al Qaeda as part of the plot. He was in the thick of it.

And then he got arrested. He was arrested on August 16th, 2001 in Minnesota where he was training on a Boeing 747 simulator as part of the plot. But even though he was in jail on September 11th, 2001, Moussaoui did his part. He did his part as a good, loyal al Qaeda soldier, he lied so that his brothers could go forward with their plan.

When he was arrested and questioned by federal agents, Moussaoui lied to them. And with that lie, his part, he caused the deaths of nearly 3,000 people, the destruction of the Trade Towers in New York, part of the Pentagon in Arlington, Virginia, and four commercial aircraft.

And he rejoiced in the death and destruction, because he knew he had done his part to kill Americans, and that the plot had succeeded. Now, he caused the deaths by lying to federal agents about what he was doing in the U.S., and his lies permitted his al Qaeda brothers to go forward, and that's what they did. That's exactly what happened.

Had Moussaoui just told the truth on August 16th and 17th, 2001, it would all have been different, and those 2,972 people, or at least some of them, would be alive today. . . .

Lies Kept Plot and Hijackers Safe

When he was arrested on August 16th and 17th, 2001, this man knew that there was a ticking bomb in the United States. He knew there was a plot about to unfold where jets would be hijacked and flown into buildings. He knew it because he was part of the plot.

And he lied to allow the plot to go forward. His lies provided the operational security to allow his brothers to go forward and kill on that horrific September morning.

The arrest and the lies. In August 2001 Moussaoui was arrested in Minnesota by federal agents. He attracted the attention of agents because he was at the Pan Am International Flight Academy, training on a Boeing 747 simulator, and he stood out because he barely knew how to fly a single engine airplane, and the other students learning how to fly a 747 were all experienced, with long aviation backgrounds.

He didn't have that. The agents suspected that he was a foreign terrorist here up to no good, and they confronted him with that. And he lied. He said no, it is a dream of mine to fly a Boeing 747 simulator. I'm just a tourist here in the United States. I'm not a terrorist. Those are lies.

They asked him about the source of his money that he used to pay for the expensive simulator training. He said: Oh, that money came from a business in England called NOP. Again, false. That money came from al Qaeda.

He told these lies instead of telling the truth, saying that he was from al Qaeda, that he was here to kill by hijacking planes, and that there were others in the United States in a plot about to unfold.

Now, what Moussaoui really knew, what he said in August 2001 was a lie. We know it is a lie and even he has now admitted it is a lie. Years after he lied, he admitted in this very courtroom that he is a terrorist. On April 22nd, 2005, he pled guilty to every one of the six charges against him in this case. Three of those charges, as the Court has told you, carry a potential sentence of death.

The Statement of Facts Reveals the Truth

When he stood before this Court and admitted his guilt, he signed a written Statement of Facts. That is an extremely important document in this case. In that Statement of Facts he told us some of what he knew about the plot, the plot to hijack planes and kill Americans. . . .

I am going to read you some of the most important parts of those admissions. . . . Paragraph 4: Moussaoui became a member of al Qaeda and pledged loyalty, a term known as bayat, to Bin Laden, whom he called his father in Jihad.

Paragraph 7: Al Qaeda members conceived of an operation in which civilian commercial airliners would be hijacked and flown into prominent buildings, including government buildings, in the United States. To effect this attack, al Qaeda associates entered the U.S., received funding from abroad, engaged in physical fitness training, and obtained knives and other weapons with which to take over airliners. Some al Qaeda associates obtained pilot training, including training on commercial jet simulators, so they would be able to fly hijacked aircraft into their targets.

Paragraph 9: Moussaoui knew of al Qaeda's plan to fly airplanes into prominent buildings in the U.S., and he agreed to travel to the U.S. to participate in the plan. Bin Laden personally selected Moussaoui to participate in the operation to fly planes into American buildings and approved Moussaoui attacking the White House. Bin Laden told Moussaoui, "Sahrawi, remember your dream." "Sahrawi," Ladies and Gentlemen, is a war name that Moussaoui used in al Qaeda.

An al Qaeda associate provided Moussaoui with information about flight schools in the United States.

Paragraph 12: On February 23rd, 2001 Moussaoui traveled to Norman, Oklahoma where he attended the Airman Flight School and received training as a pilot of smaller planes. In summer 2001 an al Qaeda associate directed Moussaoui to attend training for larger jet planes.

Paragraph 13: While in Oklahoma, Moussaoui joined a gym and bought knives. Moussaoui selected certain knives because they had blades short enough to get past airport security.

Paragraph 14: In early August 2001, an al Qaeda conspirator using the alias Ahad Sabet, wire transferred money from Germany to Moussaoui in Oklahoma so Moussaoui could receive additional flight training.

In August 2001—this is paragraph 15 now—Moussaoui trained on a Boeing 747-400 simulator at the Pan Am International Flight Academy in Eagan, Minnesota. Moussaoui told an al Qaeda associate that he would complete training before September 2001.

And paragraph 16: After his arrest, Moussaoui lied to federal agents to allow his al Qaeda brothers to go forward with the operation to fly planes into American buildings.

The Statement of Facts is a startling document. It tells us what Moussaoui knew. It tells us what Moussaoui did. And it is all the government needed to know to stop 9/11. And we will show you how.

But Moussaoui didn't give this information in August 2001. Instead, he lied, even after he was arrested, to allow his al Qaeda brothers to go forward. He lied, he told the agents none of this vital information, he told the agents none of what he later told the Court, and he and his terrorist conspirators killed people. . . .

Information to Stop the Attacks

The information shows that Moussaoui's lies killed the 9/11 victims as surely as if he had been at the controls of one of the four planes on that day.

The part of the 19 hijackers who died on September 11th, who killed innocent Americans, their part was to hijack the planes and fly them and kill Americans. Moussaoui's part, as it turned out, was to lie so they could go forward. With the information in Moussaoui's Statement of Facts from April 2005, the United States Government would have stopped the September 11th attacks, or at least saved some lives, in two ways.

One, offensively. The FBI and other government agencies would have unraveled and discovered the plot. Two, the FAA, the Federal Aviation Administration, if they had that information, would have tightened airport security and stopped the hijackers from getting on the planes that day. . . .

Now, what Moussaoui admitted in April 2005 is shocking. It is shocking for all of us to have somebody come into a courtroom like this one, stand up, proudly admit that he is a terrorist, and say that he has devoted his life to killing Americans. It is shocking to hear someone embrace evil.

But it is also shocking because it lays out the information that necessarily would have saved lives on September 11th.

But it did not. And the reason it did not is because a loyal al Qaeda soldier did his part. He did his part because when he could not pilot a plane to kill Americans, he made sure by lying that his al Qaeda brothers did.

This man, the terrorist Moussaoui, did his part. He did his part and he came in here later and told us all why, so that his al Qaeda brothers could go forward and kill Americans. Moussaoui lied so that murders could follow. He intended to kill Americans and he did.

Moussaoui acted by lying, and 2,972 people died. They were brutally murdered. He lied so his al Qaeda brothers could commit those murders and those people were killed. They were because of Moussaoui's actions.

Hold him accountable for causing those horrible deaths.

"We know that Moussaoui is an admitted al Qaeda member and that he yearns for martyrdom. . . . Please don't make him a hero."

Moussaoui Does Not Deserve to Become a Martyr

Edward MacMahon

In December 2001, Zacarias Moussaoui was indicted by a federal grand jury on multiple conspiracy charges relating to his supposed connection to the September 11, 2001, terrorist attacks against America. In 2005, Moussaoui pleaded guilty to the charges while denying his involvement with the hijackers who committed the September 11 tragedy. In March 2006 his sentencing trial began before a jury that was left to decide Moussaoui's fate. The prosecution argued that because Moussaoui claimed to know details of the September 11 attacks, he should receive the death penalty for his part in the conspiracy and for withholding information from authorities upon his arrest in August 2001 that might have prevented or minimized the ensuing tragedy. In the following opening statement before the court, Edward MacMahon, defense attorney for Moussaoui, counters that while his client indeed wanted to inflict harm against the United States, he was not part of the hijacking plot and did not have any extraordinary information that would have allowed U.S. officials to prevent the attacks from occurring.

Edward MacMahon, "Opening Statement of the Defense," *United States v. Zacarias Moussaoui*, March 6, 2006.

Consequently, MacMahon urges the jury not to sentence Moussaoui to death, arguing that this would confer upon him the status of a martyr, making him another fallen hero to inspire more suicide attacks.

Ladies and gentlemen, when we first got together in this case, Mr. Moussaoui introduced himself to you by proclaiming that he was al Qaeda and that we were all Americans. And on this point, and it may be the only one, I wholeheartedly agree with him. But his statement caused me to pause and to reflect upon who we are as a people compared to al Qaeda.

And in this case you will hear a lot about al Qaeda. Mr. Spencer [the prosecuting attorney] just told you that. You will hear a lot about its structure, its goals, and how it puts things together and how it makes operations work. And you will learn and, ladies and gentlemen, we all know that al Qaeda is a fanatic Islamic-based terror group, and we all know that their favorite weapon is suicide terrorism.

Now, what we call suicide, they call martyrdom. And martyrdom is something special to an al Qaeda member. It is just what they yearn for. They live so that they can die. Found in the luggage of Mohamed Atta [the assumed leader of the hijackers who crashed American Airlines Flight 11 into the World Trade Center North Tower] were specific instructions for the real 9/11 hijackers as to what to do and what to expect during what they called the attack that was to come.

Copies of this were found in two other people's luggage, ... but nowhere in any of the belongings of Mr. Moussaoui. I will read you a few portions of what was in this document. "When the storming begins, strike like heroes who are determined not to return to this world. Glorify Allah because this cry will strike terror in the hearts of the infidels." He said, "strike above the necks, strike all the mortals, and know that paradise has been adorned for you with the sweetest things, and the nymphs wearing their finest are calling out to you, come hither, come hither, followers of Allah."

It ends, "when the time of truth and the zero hour arrives, rip open your clothes and embrace death for the sake of Allah." . . .

This is very disturbing. But you need to keep this in mind as you hear this case. The thought of death did not deter any of the September 11th hijackers, and it won't deter any of their followers as well.

The Challenge of Fairly Judging an Enemy

And who are we? We're a nation that's governed by laws and the Constitution. We try to provide equal justice to everyone. Our Constitution guarantees to all defendants the right to a jury trial. And that is why you are here, as a check against the abuse of government power, with roots in the law as far back as the Magna Carta. And for serving we all thank you and appreciate your time.

Our Constitution also requires that persons charged with capital offenses, even admitted al Qaeda terrorists, be provided with court-appointed lawyers when they can't afford them. It is said that our justice system can only be judged by how it treats the poorest, the most despicable person who is charged with the most heinous of crimes. And if that is the case, then Moussaoui, the man behind me in the prison jumpsuit that he will wear for the rest of his life, poses the ultimate test to our legal system.

This defendant has admitted to many things. But he has not admitted any involvement in the September 11th attacks. But make no doubt, ladies and gentlemen, those attacks and the events that preceded them are the crux of this case. They form the entire heart of this case.

What the Statement of Facts contains is mostly historical admissions of a general nature about al Qaeda and its training and other plans that Moussaoui, as an admitted al Qaeda member, was in a position to know, including, yes, the existence of a plane's operation. The reason Mr. Spencer declines to tell you that he is going to prove what role Moussaoui played in the 9/11 attacks is because there is no evidence to support it.

There is no evidence as to what he did in these attacks, and the government would surely come forward with that evidence if it existed. And you will learn that before September 11th, al Qaeda was preparing many operations that involved killing Americans, and that many involved hijacking aircraft. And of those plots, the 9/11 plot was only one of them. The Statement of Facts that Moussaoui has signed contains no admission of involvement in or knowledge of the attacks that occurred on September 11th. Moussaoui certainly wasn't sent over here to tell a lie, ladies and gentlemen.

Now, the judge asked you early in this process if you could fairly judge an admitted member of al Qaeda. And this was a very difficult question. Admit to yourself, as we go through this process, ladies and gentlemen, that it will be difficult to judge your sworn enemy fairly and impartially, especially when he sits here in the courtroom with us.

We all know where we were when we learned about the attacks. We remember the shock and horror of that day. We remember the immense and senseless loss of life that occurred, as we watched, and all of us remember the incredible bravery of the police and the firemen. And we all cried that day. And we will again before this case ends, I promise you.

And we also know that the pain and losses suffered by all of the victims will never be remedied or reduced in any way by anything we do in this case. And we have all been affected by the war on terror that followed the attacks, but this trial cannot be viewed by you as jurors as part of the war on terror. This is a court of law, not a battlefield, ladies and gentlemen.

And I say to you today that we must give this man a fair trial. No matter who he is, what he thinks of us, or what he represents, this is because of who we are and what we stand for as a people and as a nation, ladies and gentlemen. And it is for this reason and many others that this trial is much more about us and who we are than it even is about him anymore.

Sentence Him Based on the Facts

So judge Moussaoui only for what he has done, on the facts and the law. You cannot judge him to get revenge for the victims or for what happened on September 11th or some substitute for [al Qaeda leader and supposed mastermind of the September 11 attacks] Usama Bin Laden.

And you must not judge him as a scapegoat for government officials who made errors before September 11th. To do so would certainly provide you an easy way to resolve the issues posed in this case. But that's the wrong approach, ladies and gentlemen. And I submit that it will lead you to the wrong verdict.

So let's look at what the evidence will be, as to actually what Moussaoui did, who he is, and in conjunction with events actually occurring in our country before September 11th. Moussaoui has pled guilty to three crimes that expose him to the death penalty. That's why we're here. But he has not admitted involvement in the attacks or that he had any knowledge about the date, the time, the targets or even the operatives in the attacks.

That information isn't set forth in the Statement of Facts, and you will hear no evidence that would support a finding in that regard. Moussaoui has admitted that he lied to the FBI when he was arrested, and those lies and the effect that they have had on our government as a whole are the central issues, that's the crux of what's happening in this portion of the case, and the issue is whether Moussaoui's lies to the FBI in August of 2001 directly caused the deaths that so tragically occurred on 9/11, just 25 days after his arrest.

I say to you that the answer to that question is no. The evidence in the case will show that nothing Moussaoui did or said, even a lie, caused anyone to die that day.

Now, there will be evidence that Moussaoui, as a sworn member of al Qaeda, was aware generally that Bin Laden was determined to attack in the United States. And there will be plenty of evidence that Moussaoui was training for some attack that involved aircraft. And there will be even more evidence of Moussaoui's stated intention to harm. He has admitted to all of that.

A Terrorist Outcast with Limited Potential

But there will be little evidence, ladies and gentlemen, that Moussaoui ever had the means or the opportunity to do anything. You will hear that he told someone of a dream he had had to attack the White House with an airplane. But those words were not matched by any action. Mr. Spencer said Moussaoui was a bad pilot. Ladies and gentlemen, he couldn't fly an airplane at all. You will hear that from their witnesses.

He talked in Oklahoma of wanting to kill infidels, but he didn't harm a soul when he was free in our country or even before. That, ladies and gentlemen, is Zacarias Moussaoui in a nutshell, sound and fury, accomplishing nothing.

I will not tell you in this case that Moussaoui wouldn't, if asked, have boarded a plane with the intention of martyring himself, on September 11th or any other day, but the evidence will be that he was intentionally isolated from the real hijackers in the United States. You will hear evidence that Moussaoui was totally useless to al Qaeda, a headache, obnoxious to everyone he encountered, and on that subject you will hear a lot of evidence, ladies and gentlemen.

You will hear from Faiz Bafana, a Muslim fundamentalist, who met Moussaoui in the year 2000. He will say that Moussaoui was, and I quote, "cuckoo in the head," that they were all relieved when he left Malaysia and was out of their hair. They even paid his ticket to get rid of him.

Now, many facts in this case will be undisputed. It is undisputed that Moussaoui was in federal custody on September 11th, where he had been for 25 days, and that before September 11th, no one in al Qaeda ever even learned that Moussaoui had been arrested. No one ever tried to call and find him. No one called to warn him to flee. And he never even tried to tell anyone that he had been arrested. So whatever role the government may say that Moussaoui played in the attacks, it was obviously so inconsequential that the attacks went forward in his absence and entirely without his participation.

How? Because the evidence will show that Moussaoui wasn't part of the plot and was ignorant of its details. Now, you will hear sufficient evidence to support Moussaoui's plea to the conspiracies in the indictment, but you will hear no evidence that will support a verdict beyond a reasonable doubt that any lie Moussaoui told in August of 2001 caused anyone to die. . . .

Moussaoui Knew What the Government Knew

Moussaoui could have told the FBI that Bin Laden was determined to strike the United States and that al Qaeda intended to hijack planes, but the government already knew that much and more. And who is to say that any government official would have believed anything that Moussaoui said anyway and launched the flawless investigation the government claims it would have launched, even then without the clues obtained in this, what we were just told is the largest criminal investigation of our history to provide the road map.

Remember, the government didn't even look for two of the hijackers. Can the government really prove beyond a reasonable doubt that it could have unraveled the 9/11 plot in 25 days in late August or early September of 2001 had Moussaoui not lied?

In closing, ladies and gentlemen, I say to you that the facts of this case will not support that verdict and the government will not prove to you beyond a reasonable doubt that anything Moussaoui did caused a death on September 11th.

We know that Moussaoui is an admitted al Qaeda member and that he yearns for martyrdom, ladies and gentlemen, but now the only way he can achieve that dream and then live on as some smiling face on a recruiting poster for Usama Bin Laden is by your verdict. Please don't make him a hero, ladies and gentlemen. He just doesn't deserve it.

*"The jurors' civic courage has probably
made all of us a little—only a little,
but still—safer."*

Moussaoui's Life Sentence Was Just

Hendrik Hertzberg

*French national Zacarias Moussaoui was arrested in the United
States and linked to the terrorist hijackers of 9/11 and to al
Qaeda. After a five-year trial in U.S. federal court, Moussaoui
was sentenced to life in prison for crimes of conspiracy. In the
following viewpoint, Hendrik Hertzberg, principal political commentator for the* New Yorker *magazine and chief speechwriter
for President Jimmy Carter during his term in office, contends
that this verdict was the only appropriate ruling the jury could
make. Hertzberg writes disparagingly about Moussaoui and his
ideas and goals, but he maintains that sentencing the al Qaeda
member to life in prison is a fate worse than death and one that
denies him martyrdom at the hands of the American legal system. Furthermore, he states that because the jury's decision was
wise and just, it will be respected by other nations—such as
France—that would have had an interest in Moussaoui's fate.*

Against the background of the chronic miasma of fear, tension, suffering, and sporadic but horrifying violence that
envelops the world on account of Islamist fundamentalist terrorism and the reaction to it, the fate of Zacarias Moussaoui,
the self-proclaimed, wanted-to-be, wasn't-there twentieth hi-

Hendrik Hertzberg, "Sentenced," *The New Yorker*, vol. 82, May 15, 2006, pp. 31–32.

jacker of September 11, 2001, is of relatively small moment. Nevertheless, a debt of gratitude is owed to the nine men and three women of the jury in Alexandria, Virginia, that declined to direct that Moussaoui be put to death. The calm seriousness with which these anonymous citizens approached their task has reassured many of us that our federal criminal-court system, even in the face of the extraordinary pressures generated by the exigencies (and the politics) of the "war on terror," remains capable of rendering justice in which sternness is guided by wisdom. And the jurors' civic courage has probably made all of us a little–only a little, but still—safer.

Moussaoui's case was a murky one. Of his criminal intentions there was never any doubt. He had toured the familiar stops on the Al Qaeda road: alienation and anomie in Europe, in his case France; fundamentalist indoctrination at the Finsbury Park mosque, in London; instruction at a terrorist camp in Afghanistan; flight training in Oklahoma and Minnesota; wire transfers of cash from abroad. But he was unstable and unreliable, and his connections to the specifics of the 9/11 plot were tenuous or nonexistent. On the day of the attacks, he was in jail awaiting deportation, having been arrested nearly a month earlier after a suspicious flight instructor tipped off the Minneapolis office of the F.B.I. His story kept changing in the course of nearly four and a half years of court proceedings, and he tried more than once to plead guilty to the conspiracy charges against him. Finally, in April of 2005, the presiding judge, Leonie Brinkema (who by all accounts conducted the case in an exemplary manner), accepted his pleas. What kept the trial going for another year was the government's fixation on pursuing the death penalty.

Global Consequences of Capital Punishment

One need feel no sympathy for Moussaoui to suspect that this fixation had more to do with domestic politics and conservative ideology than with justice per se. The familiar arguments against the death penalty apply to cases like his, some with special force. Whether or not the prospect of lethal injection deters ordinary murder—a questionable proposition at best—it is perverse to imagine that it can deter the sort of murder of which faith-based ritual suicide is an integral part. And any execution, whatever the crime it is intended to punish, degrades the society that decrees it and demoralizes the particular government employees who are assigned to carry it out. A criminal may deserve to die, may deserve even to die in terror and agony; but no civil servant deserves to be made to participate in the premeditated killing of a person who, however wicked, is on the day of execution a helpless and frightened human being.

The trial and punishment of any international terrorist occurs in a global political context that darkens another of the stains on capital punishment: the company it keeps. In 2005, according to Amnesty International, ninety-four per cent of all known executions took place in four countries. One, China, is a Communist Party dictatorship. Two others, Iran and Saudi Arabia, are Islamist autocracies. The fourth is the United States. In the democracies of Europe, American capital punishment is a source of puzzlement and disgust. But, even among Europeans who understand that its prevalence here is a function less of bloodthirstiness than of states' rights, the execution of a European national (Moussaoui is a French citizen of Moroccan descent) in a federal death chamber for a crime in which he had no direct role would have wreaked new and unnecessary damage on popular and perhaps governmental support for America's antiterrorist efforts. Moral equivalences, however false, would have been drawn, and European coöperation, which is indispensable, would have been ever so slightly undermined. The Alexandria jurors, whatever their intention, chose not to inflict that wound on their country.

After the sentence was pronounced, MSNBC trotted out a bullet-headed talk-radio host to sneer at "the sissification of

America." But if it was mercy he was deploring, his indignation was misplaced. "Life imprisonment without possibility of parole" hardly begins to describe the bleakness that awaits Moussaoui. He will be taken to the federal Supermax prison, in Florence, Colorado. He will be locked in a featureless, soundproof concrete box, seven feet by twelve. There he will remain—in solitary confinement, with scarcely a glimpse of sky and none of greenery, and no contact with other living things besides guards and insects—until he dies. The cruelty of this is terrible indeed, and any satisfaction it brings must be mixed with pity and even with shame.

The Jury Bravely Supported Justice

The Moussaoui case could have been settled long ago, with the same result and the same horrific sentence, had it not been for the government's single-minded pursuit of death. That pursuit is an apt metaphor for the wrong-headedness of what the Administration still calls, despite occasional spasms of discomfort with the term, the war on terror. The campaign against Al Qaeda in particular and Islamist terrorism in general plainly has aspects of war-fighting, but it has equally important aspects of crime-fighting and arguably more important aspects of political and ideological struggle. For the Administration, the trope of war has proved useful both for mobilizing the government and for intimidating domestic opposition, winning elections, and aggrandizing executive power. But it has also abetted the rush to the strategic disaster of Iraq and the moral disasters of Guantánamo, Abu Ghraib, and torture. Finally, it has conferred on criminal terrorists a status they desperately want but do not deserve. [Al Qaeda leader Osama] Bin Laden wished for war—war between Islam and the infidels—and war is what we gave him; Moussaoui wished for martyrdom, and our government would have granted that wish, too, if not for the jury in Virginia.

"The thought that U.S. jurors are capable of such muddled thinking is horrifying," the usually more sensible *Daily News* editorialized the day of the sentencing. "Any role in 9/11, any foreknowledge of the attacks, any aid and comfort given Al Qaeda is grounds for death. As too many forget, and as some on this jury obviously forgot, this is war." Is it? Moussaoui certainly thinks so. From the following morning's report in the *Times*:

When Robert A. Spencer, the chief prosecutor, objected that it was inappropriate for Mr. Moussaoui to make a political speech, Judge Brinkema agreed.

Mr. Moussaoui continued, nonetheless, saying, "You have branded me a terrorist or criminal." In fact, he said, he was a soldier in the Islamic cause.

In the courtroom, there was no war and there was no soldier. There was a criminal and a terrorist, and there was law and justice.

"Courtesy of the court, Moussaoui's . . . testimony has . . . been as inaccessible to the public as it would have been had Moussaoui testified before a Star Chamber."

The Media Should Have Been Allowed to Broadcast the Moussaoui Trial

John Rosenthal

When the self-proclaimed "twentieth hijacker," Zacarias Moussaoui, stood trial for his connection to the al Qaeda terrorist network and his alleged involvement in the September 11, 2001, attacks against the United States, the judge presiding over the proceedings mandated that no television network was to be allowed into the courtroom to tape and then broadcast the daily events. John Rosenthal argues in the following viewpoint that as a result of this ruling, the American people were denied the opportunity to learn more about the individuals that wish to inflict harm upon the United States as well as the mentality and teachings that inform their beliefs. Rosenthal furthermore attests that because the written transcripts of the proceedings are expensive for the public to purchase, even this avenue is closed for most Americans to discover more about terrorists and their ideology. This, Rosenthal insists, is unfortunate because Moussaoui's motivation will likely be shared by other terrorists who will strike out at the United States in the future. John Rosenthal holds a PhD in philosophy and has taught and written extensively on European politics and transatlantic relations.

John Rosenthal, "Doing Justice to Zacarias Moussaoui," *Policy Review*, vol. 146, January 2008, pp. 39–61. Copyright © 2007 Hoover Institution. Reproduced by permission.

On January 18, 2002, barely four months after the September 11 attacks, U.S. District Court judge Leonie Brinkema made a fateful ruling that would profoundly impact the public's ability to understand the nature of these attacks and of the enemy that carried them out. Rejecting motions by the television networks Court TV and C-Span, Judge Brinkema ruled that court proceedings in the case of the United States vs. suspected 9/11 co-conspirator Zacarias Moussaoui could not be broadcast in any form. The judge thereby upheld the mandatory character of a federal rule against the broadcast of judicial proceedings. She insisted, moreover, that she would have banned cameras and audio broadcasting even if the rule had not been mandatory. In a hearing on the motions, the judge pondered the petitioners' argument that the rule violated the public's constitutional right to access:

> Well, you know, this courthouse and the court reporters who will be handling this case have realtime court reporting. Which means that practically simultaneous . . . transcripts will be available of the trial proceedings. Now, that, of course, is the official record. . . . Why is that not more than sufficient to fully advise the public at large as to what is going on in the courtroom?

In her ruling, the judge then made clear that she had determined that it was. . . .

The Skewing of the Public's View

The judge did not mention, and apparently did not factor into her determination, that while transcripts would indeed be electronically available after each court session, they would only be so at a price: namely, $1 per page, with a typical trial session running into the hundreds of pages. Just how she could have imagined such an arrangement to be functionally equivalent to members of the public being able to watch the proceedings for free on cable is anybody's guess. Perhaps the judge somehow believed that print media outlets would fill the gap, purchasing transcripts and making them available to their readerships. In fact, the established media rarely published any material from the transcripts, let alone the thousands of pages comprising the complete record of the trial and pretrial proceedings.

Instead, the investment involved in purchasing and publishing transcripts was borne by a conspiracy-mongering, antigovernment website named Cryptome, which specializes in the publication of "prohibited" documents, "cryptology" (apparently the study of "secret messages"), and the exposure of "secret governance." Cryptome has also come to the attention of American law enforcement officials for publishing maps and photographs of sensitive government installations, apparently in full cognizance of the fact that the material would be of interest to terror organizations. That it would be left to a site like Cryptome to perform the obvious public service involved in making available transcripts of the Moussaoui trial is in and of itself a gauge of how thoroughly the established media failed the American public in their coverage of the case. . . .

But as the nuts-and-bolts testimony of the actual trial failed to provide any titillating revelations to support the government conspiracy thesis, the Cryptome readership apparently grew tired of the Moussaoui case. Roughly halfway through the trial proceedings, Cryptome, citing "surprisingly low reader interest and cost," ceased publication of the transcripts. Curiously—despite having already purchased well over $1,000 in Moussaoui transcripts and published tens of thousands of dollars' worth of transcripts from other terrorism-related trials—the site owner did not even see fit to reverse course two weeks later when the Cryptomites' hero, Zacarias Moussaoui, made good on his vows and dramatically took the stand in his own defense.

As a consequence, the part of the record of the Moussaoui case that is readily accessible to the public is disastrously skewed. Courtesy of the court, the bizarre ramblings in Moussaoui's pretrial motions have been freely available on the Internet for over five years now, during which time they have irrigated the fevered mental landscapes in which anti-American phantasms prosper the world over. On the other hand, and also courtesy of the court, Moussaoui's remarkably lucid and coherent testimony has, for all intents and purposes, been as inaccessible to the public as it would have been had Moussaoui testified before a Star Chamber [a secret court of law existing in England from the fifteenth to seventeenth century]. In this testimony, Moussaoui, among other things, explicitly repudiated his pretrial motions, dismissing them as, in his own words, "propaganda." "I knew that my pleadings were being put on the Internet," he explained. ". . . I carry on my propaganda war. You might not understand it, I know that some Muslim people around the world have read my pleading and have been probably motivated or happy to see that I don't give in. I fight on." . . .

Feeding the Conspiracy Theories

In light of the remarkable boom in "alternative" 9/11 conspiracy theorizing and the role of Moussaoui's own pretrial pleadings in nourishing the thesis of U.S. government foreknowledge of the attacks, a second point that is worth underscoring is that Moussaoui *explicitly rejected* this thesis on the stand. It is perhaps this fact that explains the surprising indifference to his testimony displayed by the backers of the Cryptome website. For a site specializing in the exposure of government "secrets," the most terrible "secret" is undoubtedly that the government had no secret to hide. When he returned to the stand on April 13, Moussaoui repeated his earlier characterization of his pleadings as "propaganda," explaining that they constituted for him a means of "psychological warfare." Asked about one motion in which he suggested that his apartment had been bugged by the FBI, Moussaoui dismissed it as a "fishing exercise."

Most significantly, Moussaoui explained that he truly believed following his arrest that the government might have learned that he was al Qaeda and that an attack was being prepared, because there were clues among his possessions that he thought would have tipped off investigations. But what he did not know—and, as he made clear, could not have imagined—is that as a result of the administrative "wall" separating criminal from intelligence investigations at the time, investigators were not able to search his possessions until *after* the attacks. This he learned from listening to the tragic testimony of FBI agent Harry Samit about his frantic and ultimately failed attempts to obtain first an ordinary criminal search warrant and then a FISA (Foreign Intelligence Surveillance Act) warrant. "I was not aware of . . . all this story about FISA," Moussaoui explained. "I thought that if they had access to my property, they will have searched it. So I thought . . . they were lying when they pretend they have no information. . . . I thought I could prove that the government was lying. But I was wrong because the government didn't have the right at the time to search my property."

Moussaoui's simple, straightforward explanation for the tantalizingly mysterious allusions in his pretrial statements might have helped to forestall the development of a 9/11 "Truther" movement [those who question the mainstream account of 9/11] that has in the meanwhile taken on the dimensions of a collective psychosis. But with the major media apparently uninterested and the broader public shut out from the proceedings by the broadcast ban, his testimony on the matter has hitherto passed almost wholly unperceived.

Understanding the Mind of a Terrorist

But the most fundamental lesson to be learned from Moussaoui's testimony is one that ought to have been perfectly obvious even without it: The 9/11 attacks were precisely *attacks.* They were not banal crimes actuated by banal criminal motives, as the trying of Moussaoui before an ordinary civilian jurisdiction would suggest. They were acts of war undertaken with the express purpose of inflicting damage upon a designated enemy: the United States.

Moussaoui laid out numerous particular grounds for accusing the court-appointed defense lawyers of what he styled "criminal non-assistance," but the fundamental fact of his being at war with the United States was, as he made unmistakably clear, the single overriding reason for his refusing their representation. "What on earth is the problem for the jurors to know that this defense doesn't belong to me?" he exclaimed, in defending his attempts to alert them to this fact during jury selection. "You own everything. You are America—the defense, the judge, the attackers. These people are American. I'm al Qaeda. I'm a sworn enemy of you. You, you, you, you, for me you are enemy." Apparently hoping to convince the jury that his client was delusional, [defense counsel Gerald] Zerkin repeatedly asked Moussaoui whether he thought that Zerkin himself and the other defense lawyers were part of a "conspiracy" to kill him. "In a broad sense, yes," Moussaoui responded during his March testimony, "because you are American, and I consider every American to be my enemy, so for me any American is meant to want my death because I want their death." When Zerkin attempted to press the point, asking whether the judge and jury were also part of the "conspiracy," Moussaoui interrupted him and insisted that he did not mean to refer to a conspiracy in the literal legal sense in which he himself had been charged. "When I refer to your conspiracy," he explained, "it refer to you being an American . . . so, therefore, people like me are your enemy, I'm an enemy combatant. So, in the broad sense, you are a part of this nation, so I assume that you are an enemy to me." "I want to kill American people," Moussaoui noted matter-of-factly when he took the stand again on April 13. "I believe that every American want to kill me, somehow. . . . You don't like people like me out in the street. You can't say that. You don't want somebody like me out in the street. You want me either in jail or dead."

Anyone reading Moussaoui's testimony—especially the transcript of his second appearance on the stand—could hardly doubt the wisdom of this assessment. His second appearance came on the heels of several days of emotional testimony by survivors of the 9/11 attacks and family members of victims. Asked by Zerkin whether he felt any regret for the suffering the attacks had caused them, Moussaoui answered "not whatsoever" and bluntly stated "we done it for this":

> We wanted to inflict pain on your country. . . . I'm glad they have received pain, I'm glad their family are suffering pain, and I wish there would be more pain, because I already can forecast, after tomorrow, next week, the week after, the children of Palestine will be in pain. The children of Chechnya will be in pain. . . . I want you to share in the pain. . . .

The Inadequacy of a Criminal Trial

But as Moussaoui's own words underscore—"I want to kill American people. . . . You don't want somebody like me out in the street"—even if innocent of specific charges, how could such a man be set free? A further derivative lesson of his testimony is thus the inappropriateness of a civilian jurisdiction for handling cases like that of Moussaoui. As far as al Qaeda and al Qaeda members are concerned, the 9/11 attacks were merely one "operation" in a broader and longer war on America that is ongoing. "It is a long way before we reach [get] you," Moussaoui predicted, "but we will reach you." Yet even as al Qaeda remains at war with the United States, a large part of the American political and media elite—to say nothing of their European counterparts—appear dedicated to preventing the United States from being at war with al Qaeda and taking effective action in its defense.

Criminal prosecution of al Qaeda leaders or operatives before civilian jurisdictions is clearly *not* effective action in this connection. Al Qaeda members are sworn to fight against America literally to the death. As Moussaoui explained, the preparedness to die in service to one's "emir" is the very meaning of the oath of allegiance or *bayat* that al Qaeda members have sworn to [al Qaeda leader] Osama bin Laden. It is, he said, a "death allegiance." Criminal prosecutions, even on death penalty charges, can have no dissuasive impact in this context. Especially if they are to be conducted according to the normal due process safeguards of American law, moreover, such trials involve major national security risks, the most obvious being that sworn enemies of the United States—"enemy combatants," as Moussaoui called them, willingly assuming the mantle—will go free.

If there is a category of crime under which atrocities like the 9/11 attacks could be meaningfully prosecuted, it is precisely that of *war* crimes or—per the specification for mass crimes against a civilian population introduced by the Nuremburg Tribunal—"crimes against humanity." It a curious fact, worthy of sustained reflection in its own right, that virtually none of the normally voluble champions of "international criminal law" have seen fit to accuse Osama Bin Laden or any of his lieutenants of crimes against humanity or to recommend their transfer before an international jurisdiction. But whatever exemplary or other benefit war crimes prosecutions might offer, this benefit, if it is to be sustained, is obviously predicated upon *winning the war*.

A Wasted Opportunity

I have nothing more to say because you don't want to hear the truth. It was a waste[d] opportunity for this country to understand and to know why people like me, why people like Mohammed Atta and the rest have so much hatred for you. You don't want to hear it.

These words, addressed to the Court by Zacarias Moussaoui at his sentencing hearing on May 4, 2006, provide a fitting epitaph to the trial as a whole. It was a wasted opportunity. It was not so much the opportunity to understand *why* Moussaoui and his fellow jihadists hate America that was wasted. Moussaoui's lengthy exposition on this question was undoubtedly the weakest and least compelling part of his testimony. Apart from what he called the "theological aspect"—i.e. that Islam has to be the "super power"—the rest amounted to a laundry list of sometimes fanciful grievances that clearly owed more to the well-known jeremiads [prolonged complaints] of the "anti-imperialist" western Left than to specifically Islamic sources. Although Moussaoui insisted that this second aspect derived from his "life experience," symptomatically none of the examples he gave had anything to do with the latter. The wildly exaggerated vision of American global power reflected in his remarks was itself evidently more theological than empirical in nature. How else, after all, can one explain the call to make Americans feel pain as retribution for the pain inflicted on the "children of Chechnya" by Russian troops?

The opportunity that was wasted at the Moussaoui trial was, above all, the opportunity to know and to understand that the jihadists do hate America and to appreciate the extraordinary lengths to which they are prepared to go to act on this hatred. It appears, indeed, that some Americans do not want to hear this truth: notably, the representatives of the major news organizations who served as the gatekeepers for information on the Moussaoui trial. Ironically enough, no one better exemplifies this sort of politically correct autism with regard to the Islamist threat than Judge Leonie Brinkema. Having ruled at the sentencing hearing that Moussaoui could not use his opportunity to speak in order to make a "political speech," the judge took the occasion to launch into one herself. "You came here to be a martyr and to die in a great big bang of glory," she concluded triumphantly, addressing the defendant, "but to paraphrase the poet, T.S. Elliot, instead, you will die with a whimper. The rest of your life you will spend in prison." It was as if the judge had learned nothing from the proceedings in her own courtroom over the previous four and a half years—not even the most basic and obvious fact: namely, that Zacarias Moussaoui and the other 9/11 plotters came to America to kill, not to die.

Moussaoui apparently tried to respond to Brinkema's jibe. The transcript indicates that his response was "inaudible." It is important that the words of Zacarias Moussaoui become audible to the public. Otherwise, the principled legal "victory" ostentatiously declared by Judge Brinkema might prove to be just a prelude to defeat. "We will come back another day," Moussaoui warned. There is reason to believe him.

Chapter 2

Affirming Due Process Rights for U.S. Citizens Deemed Enemy Combatants

Case Overview: *Hamdi v. Rumsfeld* (2004)

Yaser Esam Hamdi was born to Saudi Arabian parents in Louisiana in 1980. When Hamdi was young, his parents returned the family to Saudi Arabia where Hamdi was also considered a citizen. In 2001 Hamdi was picked up by Northern Alliance militia in Afghanistan during the U.S. invasion of that country. The Northern Alliance turned their captive over to American forces, which in turn sent Hamdi to the detention facility at Guantánamo Naval Base in Cuba. American officials claimed that he was fighting alongside the totalitarian Taliban regime that provided safe haven for terrorists in Afghanistan.

Once the government discovered that Hamdi was a U.S. citizen by birth, he was moved from Guantánamo to stateside military prisons. In June 2002 Hamdi's father issued a writ of habeas corpus alleging that his son was improperly detained. He claimed Hamdi was serving as a relief worker at the time of his capture. After some court wrangling, a district court judge ordered the government to produce evidence that would demonstrate Hamdi's lawful detainment. The government argued that the information was classified and appealed the court's demand. A circuit court agreed with the government and insisted that Hamdi was an enemy combatant captured in a combat zone. The court also acknowledged that because the president is invested with war powers meant to safeguard national security, the judiciary had no authority to intervene in such matters. Hamdi's father asked the U.S. Supreme Court to review the circuit court's decision, which the Court agreed to do.

In April 2004 the Supreme Court heard arguments from both sides. Government defenders cited a brief filed by a Defense Department agent who gave a description of why Hamdi was legally detained. According to the agent, Michael Mobbs, Hamdi's confinement was based on interviews that attested to his combat training, his arrest after a firefight in Afghanistan, and his relinquishing of an assault rifle at the time of his surrender. The government also maintained that the Constitution and the Authorization for Use of Military Force (AUMF—a congressional act allowing the president to use "necessary and appropriate force" against those whom he believes committed or abetted the September 11, 2001, attacks against the United States) authorize the executive branch to legally detain enemy combatants.

The Supreme Court agreed that Hamdi was legally detained under the AUMF and that Hamdi's U.S. citizenship did not exempt him from detention as an enemy combatant. Justice Sandra Day O'Connor's opinion—which, given that there was no majority ruling, stood as the Court's plurality opinion—supported Hamdi's claim that as a U.S. citizen he should be allowed due process, including a speedy trial before a "neutral decisionmaker." O'Connor also asserted that the government must present credible evidence—not merely hearsay testimony—that Hamdi is correctly classified as an enemy combatant if it intended to detain him further. In O'Connor's view, the executive cannot circumscribe judicial relief in this instance or risk intruding on civil liberties and concentrating power in only one branch of government. As she remarked, "We have long since made clear that a state of war is not a blank check for the President when it comes to the rights of the Nation's citizens." She further suggested that the government needed to create a new system of review to determine the legality of holding detainees indefinitely.

Justices Antonin Scalia and John Paul Stevens dissented from the Court's opinion. Neither took issue with the verdict that Hamdi be afforded due process. Instead, the justices argued that the president had acted unconstitutionally in detaining Hamdi. They asserted that the government could only have suspended the writ of habeas corpus (which it had not done) or tried Hamdi in a criminal court. Both men, thus, deemed O'Connor's suggestion to devise review panels as beyond the scope of the Court's authority.

Taking O'Connor's suggestion to counteract future claims of illegal detention, the White House established Combatant Status Review Tribunals (CSRTs) to ensure that all war-on-terror detainees were correctly classified as enemy combatants and therefore subject to confinement. The procedures of CSRTs and their connection to the government's attempts to deny habeas corpus relief to Guantánamo detainees, however, remained a subject of public controversy and a matter of consequence in at least two future Supreme Court cases. Meanwhile, Yaser Hamdi was returned to Saudi Arabia in late 2004 under the condition that he give up his U.S. citizenship.

"We reaffirm today the fundamental nature of a citizen's right to be free from
involuntary confinement by his own
government without due process of
law."

The Court's Decision: U.S. Citizens Detained as Enemy Combatants Must Be Afforded Due Process

Sandra Day O'Connor

In the U.S. Supreme Court case Hamdi v. Rumsfeld, *the petitioner argues that because he is a U.S. citizen, the Constitution
guarantees him the right to due process—in this case, the ability
to challenge his detainment as an enemy combatant. This case
fractured the Court, with all justices having difficulty coming to
a majority decision. Justice Sandra Day O'Connor writes on behalf of the plurality, explaining that while the government has
the ability to label a citizen an enemy combatant and hold that
person until combat with the enemy has ceased, the detained individual still has the right to challenge his status and imprisonment before an impartial party. The ruling goes on to define specific types of evidence that may or may not be admissible in
establishing an individual's guilt or innocence.*

*Justice O'Connor, the first woman appointed to the Supreme
Court, was seen as a moderate, a swing vote, assessing each case
based on its merits. She retired from the bench in January 2006.*

Sandra Day O'Connor, majority opinion, *Yaser Esam Hamdi and Esam Fouad Hamdi,
as Next Friend of Yaser Esam Hamdi, Petitioners v. Donald H. Rumsfeld, Secretary of
Defense, et al.*, June 28, 2004.

A t this difficult time in our Nation's history, we are called upon to consider the legality of the Government's detention of a United States citizen on United States soil as an "enemy combatant" and to address the process that is constitutionally owed to one who seeks to challenge his classification as such. . . . We hold that although Congress authorized the detention of combatants in the narrow circumstances alleged here, due process demands that a citizen held in the United States as an enemy combatant be given a meaningful opportunity to contest the factual basis for that detention before a neutral decisionmaker. . . .

Holding U.S. Citizens as Enemy Combatants

The threshold question before us is whether the Executive has the authority to detain citizens who qualify as "enemy combatants." There is some debate as to the proper scope of this term, and the Government has never provided any court with the full criteria that it uses in classifying individuals as such. It has made clear, however, that, for purposes of this case, the "enemy combatant" that it is seeking to detain is an individual who, it alleges, was "'part of or supporting forces hostile to the United States or coalition partners'" in Afghanistan and who "'engaged in an armed conflict against the United States'" there. We therefore answer only the narrow question before us: whether the detention of citizens falling within that definition is authorized.

The Government maintains that no explicit congressional authorization is required, because the Executive possesses plenary authority to detain pursuant to Article II of the Constitution. We do not reach the question whether Article II provides such authority, however, because we agree with the Government's alternative position, that Congress has in fact authorized Hamdi's detention, through the AUMF [Authorization for Use of Military Force]. . . .

The AUMF authorizes the President to use "all necessary and appropriate force" against "nations, organizations, or persons" associated with the September 11, 2001, terrorist attacks. There can be no doubt that individuals who fought against the United States in Afghanistan as part of the Taliban, an organization known to have supported the al Qaeda terrorist network responsible for those attacks, are individuals Congress sought to target in passing the AUMF. We conclude that detention of individuals falling into the limited category we are considering, for the duration of the particular conflict in which they were captured, is so fundamental and accepted an incident to war as to be an exercise of the "necessary and appropriate force" Congress has authorized the President to use. . . .

There is no bar to this Nation's holding one of its own citizens as an enemy combatant. In *Quirin*, [*Ex parte Quirin*, a 1942 U.S. Supreme Court case upholding U.S. military tribunals' jurisdiction over German saboteurs in the United States] one of the detainees, Haupt, alleged that he was a naturalized United States citizen. We held that "[c]itizens who associate themselves with the military arm of the enemy government, and with its aid, guidance and direction enter this country bent on hostile acts, are enemy belligerents within the meaning of . . . the law of war." While Haupt was tried for violations of the law of war, nothing in *Quirin* suggests that his citizenship would have precluded his mere detention for the duration of the relevant hostilities. . . . Nor can we see any reason for drawing such a line here. A citizen, no less than an alien, can be "part of or supporting forces hostile to the United States or coalition partners" and "engaged in an armed conflict against the United States," such a citizen, if released, would pose the same threat of returning to the front during the ongoing conflict.

In light of these principles, it is of no moment that the AUMF does not use specific language of detention. Because detention to prevent a combatant's return to the battlefield is a fundamental incident of waging war, in permitting the use of "necessary and appropriate force," Congress has clearly and unmistakably authorized detention in the narrow circumstances considered here.

Detention Until Combat Ceases

Hamdi objects, nevertheless, that Congress has not authorized the *indefinite* detention to which he is now subject. The Government responds that "the detention of enemy combatants during World War II was just as 'indefinite' while that war was being fought." We take Hamdi's objection to be not to the lack of certainty regarding the date on which the conflict will end, but to the substantial prospect of perpetual detention. We recognize that the national security underpinnings of the "war on terror," although crucially important, are broad and malleable. As the Government concedes, "given its unconventional nature, the current conflict is unlikely to end with a formal cease-fire agreement." The prospect Hamdi raises is therefore not far-fetched. If the Government does not consider this unconventional war won for two generations, and if it maintains during that time that Hamdi might, if released, rejoin forces fighting against the United States, then the position it has taken throughout the litigation of this case suggests that Hamdi's detention could last for the rest of his life.

It is a clearly established principle of the law of war that detention may last no longer than active hostilities. . . .

Hamdi contends that the AUMF does not authorize indefinite or perpetual detention. Certainly, we agree that indefinite detention for the purpose of interrogation is not authorized. Further, we understand Congress' grant of authority for the use of "necessary and appropriate force" to include the authority to detain for the duration of the relevant conflict, and our understanding is based on longstanding law-of-war principles. If the practical circumstances of a given conflict are entirely unlike those of the conflicts that informed the development of the law of war, that understanding may unravel. But that is not the situation we face as of this date. Active combat operations against Taliban fighters apparently are ongoing in Afghanistan. . . .

Due Process for Enemy Combatants

Even in cases in which the detention of enemy combatants is legally authorized, there remains the question of what process is constitutionally due to a citizen who disputes his enemy-combatant status. Hamdi argues that he is owed a meaningful and timely hearing and that "extra-judicial detention [that] begins and ends with the submission of an affidavit based on third-hand hearsay" does not comport with the Fifth and Fourteenth Amendments. The Government counters that any more process than was provided below would be both unworkable and "constitutionally intolerable." . . . Our resolution of this dispute requires a careful examination both of the writ of habeas corpus, which Hamdi now seeks to employ as a mechanism of judicial review, and of the Due Process Clause, which informs the procedural contours of that mechanism in this instance.

Though they reach radically different conclusions on the process that ought to attend the present proceeding, the parties begin on common ground. All agree that, absent suspension, the writ of habeas corpus remains available to every individual detained within the United States. . . .

The Government recognizes the basic procedural protections required by the habeas statute . . . but asks us to hold that, given both the flexibility of the habeas mechanism and the circumstances presented in this case, the presentation of the Mobbs Declaration [statement by Michael Mobbs, special advisor to the undersecretary of defense for policy, which offers the only evidence to justify Hamdi's capture and detention] to the habeas court completed the required factual development. It suggests two separate reasons for its position that no further process is due.

Government's Case Against Due Process

First, the Government urges the adoption of the Fourth Circuit's holding . . . that because it is "undisputed" that Hamdi's seizure took place in a combat zone, the habeas determination can be made purely as a matter of law, with no further hearing or factfinding necessary. This argument is easily rejected. As the dissenters from the denial of rehearing en banc [as one body] noted, the circumstances surrounding Hamdi's seizure cannot in any way be characterized as "undisputed," as "those circumstances are neither conceded in fact, nor susceptible to concession in law, because Hamdi has not been permitted to speak for himself or even through counsel as to those circumstances." . . . Further, the "facts" that constitute the alleged concession are insufficient to support Hamdi's detention. Under the definition of enemy combatant that we accept today as falling within the scope of Congress' authorization, Hamdi would need to be "part of or supporting forces hostile to the United States or coalition partners" and "engaged in an armed conflict against the United States" to justify his detention in the United States for the duration of the relevant conflict. . . . The habeas petition states only that "[w]hen seized by the United States Government, Mr. Hamdi resided in Afghanistan." . . . An assertion that one *resided* in a country in which combat operations are taking place is not a concession that one was "*captured* in a zone of active combat operations in a foreign theater of war," . . . (emphasis added), and certainly is not a concession that one was "part of or supporting forces hostile to the United States or coalition partners" and "engaged in an armed conflict against the United States." Accordingly, we reject any argument that Hamdi has made concessions that eliminate any right to further process.

The Government's second argument requires closer consideration. This is the argument that further factual exploration is unwarranted and inappropriate in light of the extraordinary constitutional interests at stake. . . . At most, the Government argues, courts should review its determination that a citizen is an enemy combatant under a very deferential "some evidence" standard. . . . Under this review, a court would assume the accuracy of the Government's articulated basis for Hamdi's detention, as set forth in the Mobbs Declaration, and assess only whether that articulated basis was a legitimate one. . . .

Balancing Public and Individual Interests

In response, Hamdi emphasizes that this Court consistently has recognized that an individual challenging his detention may not be held at the will of the Executive without recourse to some proceeding before a neutral tribunal to determine whether the Executive's asserted justifications for that detention have basis in fact and warrant in law. . . . He argues that the Fourth Circuit inappropriately "ceded power to the Executive during wartime to define the conduct for which a citizen may be detained, judge whether that citizen has engaged in the proscribed conduct, and imprison that citizen indefinitely," and that due process demands that he receive a hearing in which he may challenge the Mobbs Declaration and adduce his own counter evidence. . . .

Both of these positions highlight legitimate concerns. And both emphasize the tension that often exists between the autonomy that the Government asserts is necessary in order to pursue effectively a particular goal and the process that a citizen contends he is due before he is deprived of a constitutional right. The ordinary mechanism that we use for balancing such serious competing interests, and for determining the procedures that are necessary to ensure that a citizen is not "deprived of life, liberty, or property, without due process of law," U.S. Const., Amdt. 5, is the test that we articulated in *Mathews v. Eldridge* ... (1976) [a U.S. Supreme Court case outlining an individual's right to due process following termination of Social Security benefits].... *Mathews* dictates that the process due in any given instance is determined by weighing "the private interest that will be affected by the official action" against the Government's asserted interest, "including the function involved" and the burdens the Government would face in providing greater process. The *Mathews* calculus then contemplates a judicious balancing of these concerns, through an analysis of "the risk of an erroneous deprivation" of the private interest if the process were reduced and the "probable value, if any, of additional or substitute safeguards." ... We take each of these steps in turn.

It is beyond question that substantial interests lie on both sides of the scale in this case. Hamdi's "private interest ... affected by the official action" ... is the most elemental of liberty interests—the interest in being free from physical detention by one's own government.... "In our society liberty is the norm," and detention without trial "is the carefully limited exception." [*United States v. Salerno* (1987)]. "We have always been careful not to 'minimize the importance and fundamental nature' of the individual's right to liberty" [*Foucha v. Louisiana* (1992)] ... and we will not do so today.

Nor is the weight on this side of the *Mathews* scale offset by the circumstances of war or the accusation of treasonous behavior, for "[i]t is clear that commitment for *any* purpose constitutes a significant deprivation of liberty that requires due process protection," *Jones v. United States* ... (1983) (emphasis added; internal quotation marks omitted), and at this stage in the *Mathews* calculus, we consider the interest of the *erroneously* detained individual.... Indeed, as *amicus* briefs [briefs filed with the court by persons not parties to the case] from media and relief organizations emphasize, the risk of erroneous deprivation of a citizen's liberty in the absence of sufficient process here is very real. . . . Moreover, as critical as the Government's interest may be in detaining those who actually pose an immediate threat to the national security of the United States during ongoing international conflict, history and common sense teach us that an unchecked system of detention carries the potential to become a means for oppression and abuse of others who do not present that sort of threat. . . . Our starting point for the *Mathews v. Eldridge* analysis is unaltered by the allegations surrounding the particular detainee or the organizations with which he is alleged to have associated. We reaffirm today the fundamental nature of a citizen's right to be free from involuntary confinement by his own government without due process of law, and we weigh the opposing governmental interests against the curtailment of liberty that such confinement entails.

Allowing the Government to Fight Terror

On the other side of the scale are the weighty and sensitive governmental interests in ensuring that those who have in fact fought with the enemy during a war do not return to battle against the United States. As discussed above, the law of war and the realities of combat may render such detentions both necessary and appropriate, and our due process analysis need not blink at those realities. Without doubt, our Constitution recognizes that core strategic matters of warmaking belong in the hands of those who are best positioned and most politically accountable for making them. . . .

The Government also argues at some length that its interests in reducing the process available to alleged enemy combatants are heightened by the practical difficulties that would accompany a system of trial-like process. In its view, military officers who are engaged in the serious work of waging battle would be unnecessarily and dangerously distracted by litigation half a world away, and discovery into military operations would both intrude on the sensitive secrets of national defense and result in a futile search for evidence buried under the rubble of war. . . . To the extent that these burdens are triggered by heightened procedures, they are properly taken into account in our due process analysis.

Preserving Principles of Freedom

Striking the proper constitutional balance here is of great importance to the Nation during this period of ongoing combat. But it is equally vital that our calculus not give short shrift to the values that this country holds dear or to the privilege that is American citizenship. It is during our most challenging and uncertain moments that our Nation's commitment to due process is most severely tested; and it is in those times that we must preserve our commitment at home to the principles for which we fight abroad. . . .

We therefore hold that a citizen-detainee seeking to challenge his classification as an enemy combatant must receive notice of the factual basis for his classification, and a fair opportunity to rebut the Government's factual assertions before a neutral decisionmaker. . . . These essential constitutional promises may not be eroded.

At the same time, the exigencies of the circumstances may demand that, aside from these core elements, enemy combatant proceedings may be tailored to alleviate their uncommon potential to burden the Executive at a time of ongoing military conflict. Hearsay, for example, may need to be accepted as the most reliable available evidence from the Government in such a proceeding. Likewise, the Constitution would not be offended by a presumption in favor of the Government's evidence, so long as that presumption remained a rebuttable one and fair opportunity for rebuttal were provided. Thus, once the Government puts forth credible evidence that the habeas petitioner meets the enemy-combatant criteria, the onus could shift to the petitioner to rebut that evidence with more persuasive evidence that he falls outside the criteria. A burden-shifting scheme of this sort would meet the goal of ensuring that the errant tourist, embedded journalist, or local aid worker has a chance to prove military error while giving due regard to the Executive once it has put forth meaningful support for its conclusion that the detainee is in fact an enemy combatant. In the words of *Mathews*, process of this sort would sufficiently address the "risk of erroneous deprivation" of a detainee's liberty interest while eliminating certain procedures that have questionable additional value in light of the burden on the Government. . . .

In sum, while the full protections that accompany challenges to detentions in other settings may prove unworkable and inappropriate in the enemy-combatant setting, the threats to military operations posed by a basic system of independent review are not so weighty as to trump a citizen's core rights to challenge meaningfully the Government's case and to be heard by an impartial adjudicator.

Maintaining Checks and Balances

In so holding, we necessarily reject the Government's assertion that separation of powers principles mandate a heavily circumscribed role for the courts in such circumstances. Indeed, the position that the courts must forgo any examination of the individual case and focus exclusively on the legality of the broader detention scheme cannot be mandated by any reasonable view of separation of powers, as this approach serves only to *condense* power into a single branch of government. We have long since made clear that a state of war is not a blank check for the President when it comes to the rights of the Nation's citizens. . . . Whatever power the United States Constitution envisions for the Executive in its exchanges with other nations or with enemy organizations in times of conflict, it most assuredly envisions a role for all three branches when individual liberties are at stake. . . . Likewise, we have made clear that, unless Congress acts to suspend it, the Great

Writ of habeas corpus allows the Judicial Branch to play a necessary role in maintaining this delicate balance of governance, serving as an important judicial check on the Executive's discretion in the realm of detentions. . . . Thus, while we do not question that our due process assessment must pay keen attention to the particular burdens faced by the Executive in the context of military action, it would turn our system of checks and balances on its head to suggest that a citizen could not make his way to court with a challenge to the factual basis for his detention by his government, simply because the Executive opposes making available such a challenge. Absent suspension of the writ by Congress, a citizen detained as an enemy combatant is entitled to this process.

*"Hamdi is entitled to a habeas decree
requiring his release unless . . . criminal proceedings are promptly brought."*

Dissenting Opinion: Citizens Detained as Enemy Combatants Should Be Freed or Charged and Tried

Antonin Scalia

*Following the detention of U.S. citizen Yaser Esam Hamdi as an
enemy combatant and his demand for due process, the U.S. Supreme Court heard his case,* Hamdi v. Rumsfeld, *to decide
whether his detainment was legal and what rights an American
citizen is due when held as an enemy combatant. In his dissenting opinion, Justice Scalia argues that the ruling judges erred by
denying the petitioner the writ to habeas corpus as well as man-
dating new criteria for both the prosecuting and defending sides
to be used in determining the accuracy of the enemy combatant
categorization. Scalia holds that if a U.S. citizen is captured
while bearing arms against the United States, he must be either
charged and tried in the U.S. criminal court system or released.
Currently the second most senior justice, Scalia was appointed
his seat on the Court by President Ronald Reagan in 1986. His
rulings often represent a conservative view that values a strong
governmental and executive power.*

Antonin Scalia, dissenting opinion, *Yaser Esam Hamdi and Esam Fouad Hamdi, as
Next Friend of Yaser Esam Hamdi, Petitioners v. Donald H. Rumsfeld, Secretary of Defense, et al.*, June 28, 2004.

Where the Government accuses a citizen of waging war against it, our constitutional tradition has been to prosecute him in federal court for treason or some other crime. Where the exigencies of war prevent that, the Constitution's Suspension Clause allows Congress to relax the usual protections temporarily. Absent suspension, however, the Executive's assertion of military exigency has not been thought sufficient to permit detention without charge. No one contends that the congressional Authorization for Use of Military Force, on which the Government relies to justify its actions here, is an implementation of the Suspension Clause. Accordingly, I would reverse the [Court's] decision. . . .

Historical Understanding of Due Process

The very core of liberty secured by our Anglo-Saxon system of separated powers has been freedom from indefinite imprisonment at the will of the Executive. [Eighteenth-century English jurist Sir William] Blackstone stated this principle clearly:

"Of great importance to the public is the preservation of this personal liberty: for if once it were left in the power of any, the highest, magistrate to imprison arbitrarily whomever he or his officers thought proper . . . there would soon be an end of all other rights and immunities. . . . To bereave a man of life, or by violence to confiscate his estate, without accusation or trial, would be so gross and notorious an act of despotism, as must at once convey the alarm of tyranny throughout the whole kingdom. But confinement of the person, secretly hurrying him to gaol, where his sufferings are unknown or forgotten; is a less public, a less striking, and therefore a more dangerous engine of arbitrary government. . . .

"To make imprisonment lawful, it must either be, by process from the courts of judicature, or by warrant from some legal officer, having authority to commit to prison; which warrant must be in writing, under the hand and seal of the magistrate, and express the causes of the commitment, in order to be examined into (if necessary) upon a *habeas corpus*. If there be no cause expressed, the gaoler is not bound to detain the prisoner. For the law judges in this respect, . . . that it is unreasonable to send a prisoner, and not to signify withal the crimes alleged against him." . . .

These words were well known to the Founders. [Alexander] Hamilton, quoted from this very passage in The Federalist No. 84 [one of a series of papers arguing for ratification of the U.S. Constitution]. The two ideas central to Blackstone's understanding—due process as the right secured, and habeas corpus as the instrument by which due process could be insisted upon by a citizen illegally imprisoned—found expression in the Constitution's Due Process and Suspension Clauses.

The gist of the Due Process Clause, as understood at the founding and since, was to force the Government to follow those common-law procedures traditionally deemed necessary before depriving a person of life, liberty, or property. When a citizen was deprived of liberty because of alleged criminal conduct, those procedures typically required committal by a magistrate followed by indictment and trial. . . . The Due Process Clause "in effect affirms the right of trial according to the process and proceedings of the common law." . . .

To be sure, certain types of permissible *non*criminal detention—that is, those not dependent upon the contention that the citizen had committed a criminal act—did not require the protections of criminal procedure. However, these fell into a limited number of well-recognized exceptions—civil commitment of the mentally ill, for example, and temporary detention in quarantine of the infectious. . . . It is unthinkable that the Executive could render otherwise criminal grounds for detention noncriminal merely by disclaiming an intent to prosecute, or by asserting that it was incapacitating dangerous offenders rather than punishing wrongdoing. . . .

Aiding the Enemy Is a Criminal Offense

The allegations here, of course, are no ordinary accusations of criminal activity. Yaser Esam Hamdi has been imprisoned because the Government believes he participated in the waging of war against the United States. The relevant question, then, is whether there is a different, special procedure for imprisonment of a citizen accused of wrongdoing *by aiding the enemy in wartime.*

Justice [Sandra Day] O'Connor, writing for a plurality of this Court, asserts that captured enemy combatants (other than those suspected of war crimes) have traditionally been detained until the cessation of hostilities and then released. That is probably an accurate description of wartime practice with respect to enemy *aliens.* The tradition with respect to American citizens, however, has been quite different. Citizens aiding the enemy have been treated as traitors subject to the criminal process.

As early as 1350, England's Statute of Treasons made it a crime to "levy War against our Lord the King in his Realm, or be adherent to the King's Enemies in his Realm, giving to them Aid and Comfort, in the Realm, or elsewhere." . . .

Subjects accused of levying war against the King were routinely prosecuted for treason. . . . The Founders inherited the understanding that a citizen's levying war against the Government was to be punished criminally. The Constitution provides: "Treason against the United States, shall consist only in levying war against them, or in adhering to their Enemies, giving them Aid and Comfort"; and establishes a heightened proof requirement (two witnesses) in order to "convic[t]" of that offense. . . .

The modern treason statute is 18 U.S.C. § 2381 it basically tracks the language of the constitutional provision. Other provisions of Title 18 criminalize various acts of warmaking and adherence to the enemy. . . . The only citizen other than Hamdi known to be imprisoned in connection with military hostilities in Afghanistan against the United States *was* subjected to criminal process and convicted upon a guilty plea [namely, John Walker Lindh, captured alongside other Taliban fighters in November 2001]. . . .

Suspending Habeas Corpus

There are times when military exigency renders resort to the traditional criminal process impracticable. English law accommodated such exigencies by allowing legislative suspension of the writ of habeas corpus for brief periods. . . .

Our Federal Constitution contains a provision [the Suspension Clause] explicitly permitting suspension, but limiting the situations in which it may be invoked: "The privilege of the Writ of Habeas Corpus shall not be suspended, unless when in Cases of Rebellion or Invasion the public Safety may require it." Although this provision does not state that suspension must be effected by, or authorized by, a legislative act, it has been so understood, consistent with English practice and the Clause's placement in Article 1.

The Suspension Clause was by design a safety valve, the Constitution's only "express provision for exercise of extraordinary authority because of a crisis." . . . Very early in the Nation's history, President [Thomas] Jefferson unsuccessfully sought a suspension of habeas corpus to deal with Aaron Burr's conspiracy to overthrow the Government. . . . During the Civil War, Congress passed its first Act authorizing Executive suspension of the writ of habeas corpus, . . . to the relief of those many who thought President [Abraham] Lincoln's unauthorized proclamations of Suspension . . . unconstitutional. Later Presidential proclamations of suspension relied upon the congressional authorization, *e.g.*, Proclamation No. 7, 13 Stat. 734 (1863). During Reconstruction, Congress passed the Ku Klux Klan Act, which included a provision authorizing suspension of the writ, invoked by President [Ulysses S.] Grant in quelling a rebellion in nine South Carolina counties. . . .

Hamdi Should Have Access to Habeas Corpus

It follows from what I have said that Hamdi is entitled to a habeas decree requiring his release unless (1) criminal proceedings are promptly brought, or (2) Congress has suspended the writ of habeas corpus. A suspension of the writ could, of course, lay down conditions for continued detention, similar to those that today's opinion prescribes under the Due Process Clause. But there is a world of difference between the people's representatives' determining the need for that suspension (and prescribing the conditions for it), and this Court's doing so.

The plurality finds justification for Hamdi's imprisonment in the Authorization for Use of Military Force, 115 Stat. 224, which provides:

"That the President is authorized to use all necessary and appropriate force against those nations, organizations, or persons he determines planned, authorized, committed, or aided the terrorist attacks that occurred on September 11, 2001, or harbored such organizations or persons, in order to prevent any future acts of international terrorism against the United States by such nations, organizations or persons."

This is not remotely a congressional suspension of the writ, and no one claims that it is. Contrary to the plurality's view, I do not think this statute even authorizes detention of a citizen with the clarity necessary to satisfy the interpretive canon that statutes should be construed so as to avoid grave constitutional concerns, . . . or with the clarity necessary to overcome the statutory prescription that "[n]o citizen shall be imprisoned or otherwise detained by the United States except pursuant to an Act of Congress." . . . But even if it did, I would not permit it to overcome Hamdi's entitlement to habeas corpus relief. The Suspension Clause of the Constitution, which carefully circumscribes the conditions under which the writ can be withheld, would be a sham if it could be evaded by congressional prescription of requirements *other than com-*

mon law requirement of committal for criminal prosecution that render the writ, though available, unavailing. If the Suspension Clause does not guarantee the citizen that he will either be tried or released, unless the conditions for suspending the writ exist and the grave action of suspending the writ has been taken; if it merely guarantees the citizen that he will not be detained unless Congress by ordinary legislation says he can be detained; it guarantees him very little indeed.

The Plurality's "Mr. Fixit" Mentality

It should not be thought, however, that the plurality's evisceration of the Suspension Clause augments, principally, the power of Congress. As usual, the major effect of its constitutional improvisation is to increase the power of the Court. Having found a congressional authorization for detention of citizens where none clearly exists; and having discarded the categorical procedural protection of the Suspension Clause; the plurality then proceeds, under the guise of the Due Process Clause, to prescribe what procedural protections *it* thinks appropriate. It "weigh[s] the private interest . . . against the Government's asserted interest," . . . and—just as though writing a new Constitution—comes up with an unheard-of system in which the citizen rather than the Government bears the burden of proof, testimony is by hearsay rather than live witnesses, and the presiding officer may well be a "neutral" military officer rather than judge and jury. . . . It claims authority to engage in this sort of "judicious balancing" from *Mathews v. Eldridge* (1976), a case involving . . . *the withdrawal of disability benefits!* Whatever the merits of this technique when newly recognized property rights are at issue (and even there they are questionable), it has no place where the Constitution and the common law already supply an answer.

Having distorted the Suspension Clause, the plurality finishes up by transmogrifying [changing the appearance of] the Great Writ—disposing of the present habeas petition by remanding for the District Court to "engag[e] in a factfinding process that is both prudent and incremental," . . . "In the absence of [the Executive's prior provision of procedures that satisfy due process], . . . a court that receives a petition for a writ of habeas corpus from an alleged enemy combatant must itself ensure that the minimum requirements of due process are achieved." . . . This judicial remediation of executive default is unheard of. The role of habeas corpus is to determine the legality of executive detention, not to supply the omitted process necessary to make it legal. . . . It is not the habeas court's function to make illegal detention legal by supplying a process that the Government could have provided, but chose not to. If Hamdi is being imprisoned in violation of the Constitution (because without due process of law), then his habeas petition should be granted; the Executive may then hand him over to the criminal authorities, whose detention for the purpose of prosecution will be lawful, or else must release him.

There is a certain harmony of approach in the plurality's making up for Congress's failure to invoke the Suspension Clause and its making up for the Executive's failure to apply what it says are needed procedures—an approach that reflects what might be called a Mr. Fix-it Mentality. The plurality seems to view it as its mission to Make Everything Come Out Right, rather than merely to decree the consequences, as far as individual rights are concerned, of the other two branches' actions and omissions. Has the Legislature failed to suspend the writ in the current dire emergency? Well, we will remedy that failure by prescribing the reasonable conditions that a suspension should have included. And has the Executive failed to live up to those reasonable conditions? Well, we will ourselves make that failure good, so that this dangerous fellow (if he is dangerous) need not be set free. The problem with this approach is not only that it steps out of the courts' modest and limited role in a democratic society; but that by repeatedly doing what it thinks the political branches ought to do it encourages their lassitude and saps the vitality of government by the people. . . .

Balancing Safety and Freedom

The Founders well understood the difficult tradeoff between safety and freedom. "Safety from external danger," Hamilton declared,

"is the most powerful director of national conduct. Even the ardent love of liberty will, after a time, give way to its dictates. The violent destruction of life and property incident to war; the continual effort and alarm attendant on a state of continual danger, will compel nations the most attached to liberty, to resort for repose and security to institutions which have a tendency to destroy their civil and political rights. To be more safe, they, at length, become willing to run the risk of being less free." . . .

The Founders warned us about the risk, and equipped us with a Constitution designed to deal with it.

Many think it not only inevitable but entirely proper that liberty give way to security in times of national crisis—that, at the extremes of military exigency, *inter arma silent leges* ["among (times of) arms the laws fall mute"]. Whatever the general merits of the view that war silences law or modulates its voice, that view has no place in the interpretation and application of a Constitution designed precisely to confront war and, in a manner that accords with democratic principles, to accommodate it. Because the Court has proceeded to meet the current emergency in a manner the Constitution does not envision, I respectfully dissent.

"The state of civil liberties in the United States is only worse as a result of [the Hamdi] ruling."

Hamdi Diminishes Citizens' Civil Rights

Mel Lipman

In Hamdi v. Rumsfeld, *the plurality opinion of the U.S. Supreme Court held that while an American citizen could be held by the government as an enemy combatant, that person must be granted the right to due process to challenge his detention. Although many observers believed the ruling upheld the rights guaranteed to all citizens by the Constitution, Nevada civil liberties attorney Mel Lipman contends in the following viewpoint that when examined closely, the ruling actually undercuts these rights by placing the burden of proof upon the defendant and by exemplifying the Court's unwillingness to check the executive branch's assumed power to hold citizens indefinitely without trial. Lipman also fears that the touted victory for civil liberties will falsely give Americans the impression that the administration's imperialist claims have finally been stymied by the courts. Besides serving as an attorney, Mel Lipman is the president of the American Humanist Association, which seeks to defend constitutional liberties and which advocates for progressive social change.*

The Supreme Court's [2004] decision in the *Hamdi v. Rumsfeld* case regarding the detention of an American citizen as an "enemy combatant," along with its sister cases, is

Mel Lipman, "Guilty Until Proven Innocent: What's Missing in the Analysis of the *Hamdi* Ruling," *Humanist*, vol. 64, September 2004, pp. 42–43. Copyright © 2004 American Humanist Association. Reproduced by permission.

being hailed positively as the most significant civil liberties opinion in a half century. While the importance is undeniable, many organizations and news outlets mischaracterize the *Hamdi* ruling as a landmark decision in defense of the Bill of Rights. It is not.

After reading so many headlines declaring victory for civil liberties and defeat for the [George W.] Bush administration, one can't help wondering if anyone actually read the opinions. One simple demonstration of the lack of critical reporting on this case is that nearly every news source from National Public Radio to the *Washington Times* reported the vote on the ruling as 8-1 when in fact it was 6-3, as even a casual reading of the opinions confirms.

Ignoring the Negative Details

Key elements of the *Hamdi* decision are glaringly absent from favorable reviews. First, the Court ruled that lower courts which hear detainee cases must shift the focal point away from the merits of the case and limit the right to fair trial by focusing only on whether the person was correctly labeled an enemy combatant. Second, the trial the Court demands turns the U.S. legal system on its head by forcing the accused to prove his or her innocence. Third, the trial described in the ruling is stripped of its usual protections against hearsay, giving nearly all the cards to the executive branch attorneys.

In reworking an important part of the U.S. government's system of checks and balances, the power of the executive branch has been inappropriately expanded. Because of this our civil liberties would be better served if there had been no decision. This opinion is a step backward that will excuse long-term imprisonments for U.S. citizens with no right to a fair trial addressing the merits of their cases.

Yes, it could have been worse. To the Court's credit the majority rightly recognized and ruled that the right to habeas corpus, absent suspension of that right by Congress, cannot be denied and that persons labeled as "enemy combatants" have the right to challenge, in front of a neutral decision maker, the government's evidence used to declare them as such.

Unfortunately, in the limited nature of this ruling, the majority justices overlooked the severity of the harm done when potentially innocent citizens can be imprisoned until the "end of hostilities," (perhaps indefinitely, considering the nature of the so-called war on terror) without a trial that truly addresses the merits of their alleged crimes.

The Possibility of Indefinite Detention

Missing from public analysis of the decision is the way in which the Court established a new standard of "guilty until proven innocent." In an attempt to balance the competing interests of the individual and the government, the Court decided that the burden of proof would be on the defendant, who would have to show that the government's evidence was wrong or insufficient to declare him or her an enemy combatant. The Court also ruled that the government is granted to lower standards for evidence, specifically allowing it to introduce hearsay with the presumption of truth. It is hard to imagine a more egregious departure from the long-celebrated legal cornerstone of "innocent until proven guilty."

The Court fails to clarify its position on the potential for long-term, even lifelong, detention. Indeed, in her opinion, Justice Sandra Day O'Connor acknowledges that given the broad nature of the "war on terror" it could become very difficult to determine when the conflict has ended, resulting in a prolonged detention once a person is recognized as an enemy combatant.

But even the pseudo trial that the Court demands need not be held until a significant internment had already taken place. O'Connor neglects to remedy this problem and in fact leaves the door open for prolonged detainment by stating that the trial over whether or not the government is correct in its assertion that the accused is an "enemy combatant" is "only due when the determination is made to continue to hold those who have been seized." It is dangerously unclear when the "continue to" threshold would be crossed.

Further, there is no indication in the opinion that existing domestic and international law regarding detentions will be followed. For one example, Congress' own USA PATRIOT Act allows detentions of aliens for no longer than seven days. In his dissent, Justice David Souter lends credence to this concern when he writes, "There is reason to question whether the United States is acting in accordance with the laws of war it claims to follow."

For another example, the Supreme Court ruling states that these detained "enemy combatants" may challenge their internment, but Ali Seleh Marri, a Qatar native who has been held for over a year at the Charleston Naval Consolidated Brig on charges of credit card and bank fraud, hasn't been allowed to see his attorney. Marri, who had originally been scheduled to go to trial [in 2003], until his prosecutors dropped the charges, was then designated an enemy combatant by the government. Marri's attorneys, citing the Supreme Court decision, asked in early July [2004] Assistant Solicitor General David Salmons to see their client and were then told that, according to the motion, the government would still not allow Marri to see a lawyer.

Increasing the Power of the Executive

Overall, with this ruling the Court has damaged the constitutional right to a fair and speedy trial by creating separate standards, both for what the right to due process means and for what the trial must entail. Considering the nature of this decision, it is clear that when O'Connor writes, "We affirm today the fundamental nature of a citizen's right to be free from involuntary confinement" she overstates the Court's far more limited achievement.

While we're still hearing praise about this case from liberal quarters, the real story is that the *Hamdi* ruling has increased the power of the Executive, giving Bush just shy of everything he wanted. Since September 11, 2001, we seem to be witnessing the sad crumbling of the U.S. system of checks and balances. First Congress abdicated responsibility by giving the president carte blanche to make war whenever and wherever he wishes and now the Supreme Court has relinquished its responsibility to protect individual liberties. Clearly, Monday, June 28, [2004,] was a somber day for civil liberties, and one made even more dour by the fact that so few even noticed the setback.

The state of civil liberties in the United States is only worse as a result of this ruling. Before the decision, public concern was rising to a high point about the way the administration was improperly detaining U.S. citizens indefinitely. Now concern is lessened as the executive branch continues to do the same thing, pausing only to undertake the formalities of a trial rigged against the detainee.

> *"Any individual whom the government holds in custody ... should be able to test the legality of that custody as a matter of human rights, not citizenship."*

Due Process Protections Should Extend to Noncitizens

Peter H. Shuck

In the following essay, Yale Law School professor and author of numerous books on topics such as immigration and citizenship, Peter H. Shuck, writes that the Hamdi v. Rumsfeld *ruling was unique among the court cases of enemy combatants challenging their detention at the hands of the U.S. government because in* Hamdi *the petitioner was a U.S. citizen. Shuck explains how citizenship is obtained and some of the rights it confers. As Shuck emphasizes, Yaser Hamdi, the petitioner in the case, was granted the privilege of due process, but this right was afforded him by the Supreme Court only because of the fact that he was born in the United States. Shuck contends that this privilege of citizenship may be outdated in a world that is becoming increasingly interconnected, and he suggests that the right to due process might be better conceived of as a human right, one that could be shared by all those who are held without trial.*

The U.S. Supreme Court's decisions in *Rasul v. Bush* and *Hamdi v. Rumsfeld* concerning the hearing rights of terrorism suspects detained at Guantanamo and in the United States have received much public attention, and deservedly so.

By anyone's definition, these are landmark decisions—both for their holdings and for their supporting rhetoric about constitutional limits on the commander in chief during wartime. Less obvious but equally important, the decisions cast a spotlight on the status of American citizenship in the post-9/11 world.

One little-noted feature of the Court's analysis was its differential treatment of the U.S. citizen detainee, [Yaser] Hamdi, and the noncitizen detainees in Guantanamo. Although the Court did not prescribe in detail the kinds of hearings to which the two groups are entitled [and was especially cryptic about the nature of the Guantanamo hearings], it seems clear that citizens like Hamdi will be able to claim more procedural protections than noncitizens can. This may be true, moreover, whether the detainees are held onshore or abroad—although this is less certain. Also left open is the role that defense lawyers will be allowed to play during prehearing interrogations. Here too, however, citizens are likely to have more extensive rights than noncitizens.

This difference raises basic questions about the nature and meaning of citizenship. Why does the law distinguish between citizens and noncitizens at all? For which purposes should it do so, and with what legal consequences? More specifically, should detainees' procedural rights turn on their citizenship? And most fundamentally, who should answer these questions—the U.S. Congress? The courts? The military? International tribunals?

Questions like these are particularly vexing in the case of a citizen such as Hamdi. Born in the U.S., Hamdi left with his family for Saudi Arabia as a child, never [so far as we know] to return until seized on the battlefield in Afghanistan and brought here for interrogation and processing as an enemy combatant. Assuming that citizens can claim greater rights than noncitizens, is Hamdi—a man with no apparent links to the U.S. other than the accident of birth here—the kind of citizen who should receive them? The Constitution's answer appears to be yes.

Four Relevant Aspects of Citizenship

Four aspects of citizenship are most relevant to cases like *Hamdi*: acquisition, duality, loss, and differential rights.

Acquisition. Most countries today base their citizenship, at least in part, on the jus soli [or birthright] principle—the idea that with very minor exceptions, anyone born on its territory is, simply by virtue of that fact, a citizen. Even some nations like Germany that traditionally limited citizenship to those with a common ethnicity have recently added certain jus soli elements. The U.S., however, has the most expansive version of jus soli citizenship, extending it even to the native-born children of illegal aliens and temporary visitors, however briefly either the mother or the native-born child is here—in the Hamdis' case, not very long. For those not born in the U.S., naturalization is also relatively simple, requiring only five years' legal residency [three if married to a citizen], good moral character, and the most rudimentary knowledge of the English language and American government. Under the principle of jus sanguinis [law of descent], foreign-born children of an American parent can often acquire citizenship without meeting even these standards.

Dual Citizenship. Easy acquisition of U.S. citizenship, combined with nationality laws of other countries and cross-national intermarriage, makes dual or even triple citizenship increasingly common. The children of such marriages who are born in the U.S. often enjoy both American citizenship through birth and their parents' citizenship[s] by descent. Hamdi, for example, was an American citizen by birth in the U.S. and a Saudi citizen by descent from his parents. In addition, although immigrants naturalizing here must renounce their earlier allegiances, their countries of origin may decide to treat such renunciations as legally ineffective, in which case they retain their original [renounced] nationalities as well as their new American one. In the past, the U.S. government discouraged dual nationality, seeing it as a potential source of conflicts of loyalty, diplomatic disputes, and other problems. Today, however the government is resigned to it.

Loss of Citizenship. If American citizenship is easy to acquire, it is also difficult to lose—unless the citizen intentionally expatriates himself in a formal document before a government official. Beginning in 1907, Congress enacted provisions that denationalized U.S. citizens who committed specified acts. [A woman's acquiring a foreign nationality through marriage was one such act, an egregiously/discriminatory provision upheld by the Supreme Court but later repealed by Congress.] Expatriating acts included such conduct as naturalizing in or declaring allegiance to a foreign country, voting in a foreign election, deserting the U.S. military in a time of war, avoiding military service during wartime by leaving or remaining outside the country, returning to and living in one's country of origin for a certain period after having naturalized in the U.S., serving in a foreign government, and, of course, treason. In a zigzag series of denationalization decisions culminating in the 1967 case of *Afroyim v. Rusk*, the Supreme Court developed a rule that denies Congress any power to deprive a citizen of his citizenship without his consent. This rule, now codified in statute, limits denationalization to the rare situation in which one commits a legally defined expatriating act with a specific intent to relinquish citizenship.

Differential Rights. Traditionally, federal and much state law allowed government and employers to favor citizens over noncitizens in the allocation of public benefits and jobs. This was justified on the theory [to the extent one was articulated] that these were discretionary privileges, not rights, and that visitors had weaker claims on them than citizens did. Supreme Court decisions, however, gradually limited the states' power to discriminate against noncitizens; in 1971 the Court rejected a state law denying noncitizens otherwise available welfare benefits. Thereafter, the law tended to minimize the differences between the legal rights [and duties, which are minimal in both cases] of citizens and noncitizens. I have termed this a "devaluation" of citizenship and argued that, although this reduced immigrants' incentives to naturalize, it was on balance desirable that the law treated citizens and noncitizens largely the same. [The main exceptions were the citizens' right to vote, their higher priority in bringing close relative immigrants to the U.S., and their eligibility for some public jobs barred to noncitizens.] In 1996 Congress seemed to "revalue" citizenship by enacting a welfare reform law that limited noncitizens' access to a number of federally funded benefit programs—a discrimination later upheld by the courts. Within a few years, however, Congress restored some of these benefits, and most of the high-immigration states used their own funds to replace some of the withdrawn support, so that most [though not all] legal immigrants can now claim much the same basic benefits that their citizen counterparts enjoy.

Intellectual Critique of Citizenship

For almost all Americans, the idea of an exclusive national citizenship, one that draws a sharp line between members and nonmembers and treats the latter unequally in certain respects, is unexceptionable. To many, this idea is part of what it means to be an American. Fairness, in this conventional view, requires only that U.S. citizenship be available on easy terms to all long-term immigrants on a nondiscriminatory basis.

In contrast, however, many intellectuals who write about citizenship take a different view: They oppose pretty much any discrimination against noncitizens. The big exception is the right to vote, but even here many academics propose that noncitizens be allowed to vote, particularly in local or special-purpose [e.g., school board] elections, as permitted in many

European and some American communities. The intellectual critique of traditional citizenship is of three types: egalitarian, functional, and transnational.

Egalitarian. In the egalitarian view, very common among academics, status differentials are presumptively illegitimate, especially when government mandates them. Even more objectionable are differentials that correlate with and disadvantage racial and ethnic minorities, as is the case with the citizen-noncitizen distinction. These inequalities, the argument runs, are like suspect classifications in equal protection jurisprudence; they must be narrowly tailored and can be justified, if at all, only by compelling reasons. In addition, many egalitarians, drawing on the work of the English social theorist T.H. Marshall, maintain that the legal-political conception of citizenship is radically incomplete. In this view, a robust citizenship requires a level of economic and social equality necessary for full participation in public and private life.

Functional. Another critique of traditional citizenship emphasizes that noncitizens are hardworking, pay taxes, and obey the laws [at least those in legal status do], just as citizens do. Given this functional equality, the argument goes, noncitizens should enjoy the same rights as citizens. Academics often extend this argument to undocumented workers, noting the unfairness of the fact that these workers pay the same payroll, sales, and indirect taxes as others do but are not in a position, because of their illegal status, to claim Social Security and other benefits that their taxes help finance.

Transnational. To many commentators, the traditional notion of citizenship, organized around the nation-state, is increasingly anachronistic. Human rights advocates cite the growing number of international conventions that recognize universal rights—for example, protections against torture, persecution, discrimination, and environmental insults—that individuals can claim as human beings rather than as members of a particular national polity. Others point to the growth of supranational institutions such as the European Union, World Trade Organization, United Nations, International Criminal Court, and many regional groupings such as NAFTA [North American Free Trade Agreement] that exercise real power over individuals and nations. Multinational corporations and international nongovernmental organizations [NGOs] transcend national borders and allegiances. Even ordinary individuals are educated, work, invest, and consume in a global market that is increasingly/shaped by forces over which any single nation, even the U.S., has relatively little control. In this environment, many academics think, it makes little sense for people's basic rights to vary simply by virtue of their nationality.

Citizenship Post-9/11

How, then, should we think about the nature and law of citizenship, post-9/11? The most important fact in our new world is that the main risk to our national security, which until 9/11 seemed to exist only abroad, is now domestic, indeed local [especially for New York and Washington, D.C.]. This risk can be contained only by intensive intelligence-gathering and by screening of people in public places, often on the basis of statistical profiles that inevitably produce some false positives.

Should all U.S. citizens be automatically exempted from this screening, just as they can now avoid long lines and interrogation at airports and other ports of entry? Does the fact that the Oklahoma City bombers turned out to be U.S. citizens mean that citizenship is not a good screening criterion, that noncitizen status is poor proxy for the risk of terrorism? These questions are complicated by legal roles that confer full citizenship on people like Hamdi who were born here but have no other ties to or stake in the U.S., and that give noncitizens fewer rights, both procedural [as *Hamdi* and *Rasul* seem to imply] and substantive [as the 1996 welfare law provides].

Citizenship is a broad legal category bearing rights that Congress may not constitutionally subdivide. In a 1964 decision, *Schneider v. Rusk*, the Court overturned a law that treated birthright and naturalized citizens differently, and under this principle, Congress may lack power to disadvantage birthright citizens like Hamdi just because they moved abroad at an early age and became strangers. [Interestingly, Hamdi has agreed to renounce his U.S. citizenship in return for being released and deported to Saudi Arabia.]

In contrast, Congress has broad discretion to regulate naturalization standards. Would it increase the nation's security or unity by requiring applicants for post-9/11 citizenship to demonstrate greater knowledge about, and loyalty and commitment to, American life than the law required in the past? This is an important question for us to debate. In my view, we should resist the temptation to toughen naturalization by imposing new tests of loyalty and commitment. For birthright citizens like Hamdi who lived among us only briefly and long ago severed any ties to our society, membership should perhaps lapse at some point. But any individual whom our government holds in custody, whether citizen or stranger, should be able to test the legality of that custody as a matter of human rights, not citizenship.

> "New categories of criminality like en-
> emy combatants or domestic terrorists
> are invented and imposed on the body
> politic [by Hamdi]."

Hamdi Sets a Dangerous Precedent

Marc Norton

As Marc Norton writes in the following viewpoint, the ruling in
Hamdi v. Rumsfeld, *involving the rights of a U.S. citizen detained as an enemy combatant, had far-reaching consequences
for the future treatment of individuals held by the government.
Norton contends that the gravest consequence of the* Hamdi *ruling is the establishment of the term "enemy combatant" within
the U.S. legal system. Specifically, he notes that since the ruling
in the case supported the government's assumed power to label
citizens as enemy combatants based on flimsy evidence, all citizens are at a greater risk of being wrongly held captive by the
government. Marc Norton has written extensively on the categorization of enemy combatant in several liberal publications such
as* Covert Action Quarterly, CounterPunch.org, *and* Beyond-
Chron, *a daily online newspaper based in San Francisco.*

From now on, anybody deemed an enemy combatant—
citizen and non-citizen alike—can be imprisoned and
stripped of their constitutional "due process" rights, including
the presumption of innocence and the right to a jury trial. Indefinite detention remains an option. The military will be
running the show, not the courts.

Marc Norton, "The Supreme Court and 'Enemy Combatants,'" *Marc Norton Online*,
Spring 2005. Copyright © 2005 Covert Action Publications, Inc. Reproduced by permission.

A few more victories like this, and we will all be eating prison gruel. . . .

Inventing the Enemy Combatant

In the immediate aftermath of 9/11, immigrants from Arab Muslim countries were subjected to a series of federal round-ups. Hundreds, if not thousands, were jailed without charges, held incommunicado for unknown periods of time in unknown places. Many of those rounded-up were later deported. There is still no complete and accurate record of these detainees. Thousands more were targeted for "voluntary" interviews and investigations. Many thousands more were subjected to a "special registration" campaign that produced yet more arrests and deportations. FBI director Robert Mueller set "specific numerical goals" for "terrorism investigations," based on the number of mosques in given communities—this from a representative of the same political trend that opposes affirmative action. There was open talk of the need for torture of terrorism suspects.

Congress, for its part, rushed through the passage of the Patriot Act. This act, among its many transgressions on the Constitution and the Bill of Rights, included the creation of the new crime of "domestic terrorism."

The Patriot Act defines a domestic terrorist as someone who commits "acts dangerous to human life that are a violation of the criminal laws . . . [and] that appear to be intended . . . to influence the policy of a government by intimidation or coercion." Many have argued that this broad definition would make terrorists even of [civil rights activists] Martin Luther King and Rosa Parks. After all, civil disobedience often provokes a response that is "dangerous to human life," nearly always involves violating the law, and is certainly intended "to influence the policy of a government." Of course, "intimidation or coercion" are in the eye of the beholder.

As yet, no individual has actually been prosecuted as a domestic terrorist under the Patriot Act. But the creation of the new category of "domestic terrorist," propagated by the media far and wide, coupled with the ongoing anti-immigrant hysteria, helped lay the ideological groundwork for yet another invented category of criminality, the "enemy combatant."

The concept of enemy combatants did not emerge from any legislation. It sprung instead from the seeds of war sown in the fields of Afghanistan. By the time the U.S.-made Taliban [the restrictive government of Afghanistan in place because of earlier U.S. actions] was driven out of the cities of that war-torn nation, the U.S. found itself holding many hundreds of prisoners. In one of those quaint wars from the 20th century, these prisoners would have been sent to camps for prisoners-of-war. They would have been given the minimal protections of the Geneva Conventions, at least in theory, including the right not to be forcefully interrogated. . . .

Before long, the prisoners rounded up in Afghanistan were being sent thousands of miles away to Guantanamo Bay, a U.S. military base in Cuba illegally occupied for over a century. The world was presented with more graphic images of prisoners, hog-tied and blindfolded, sent off to open-air cages, treated little better than animals in the zoo. . . .

In Guantanamo, it was readily apparent to the whole world that the Geneva Conventions were being flagrantly violated. As protests mounted about the incarceration and treatment of the Guantanamo prisoners, it became necessary for the U.S. to develop some excuse for its lawlessness. Thus the concept of enemy combatants.

For sure, there had been individuals incarcerated in previous U.S. wars, and afforded less than due process. The pundits supporting the barbarity of Guantanamo have been quick to cite any example they could. For those with some historical memory, the example of the Japanese interned during World War II comes readily to mind, although most of the [George

W.] Bush regime's apologists have stayed away from any discussion of that disgraceful case-in-point.

But, historical examples be what they may, the category of enemy combatants was brand new. You can't find this term in any law book, not even in the Patriot Act. But the corporate media, glad to make one of its many contributions to the "war on terror," collaborated with the Bush regime to make up and insert this new category into the political discourse, much like Winston Smith in George Orwell's *1984* [an English novel about life in a nightmarish dictatorship] creating history from his desk at the Ministry of Truth.

The Bush regime's new concept of enemy combatants was breathtaking. As it evolved, it gradually became clear that Bush was claiming the authority to unilaterally declare anyone, anywhere in the world, to be an enemy combatant, and consequently strip them of all rights afforded them by the constitution, by international law, or by any law whatsoever. No assertion of authority could have been more absolute.

Citizen Enemy Combatants

Still, given the way things work in the U.S., the legal black hole in Guantanamo caused barely a ripple in the body politic. Those disappeared in plain sight in Cuba are, after all, foreigners. U.S. politics is so fundamentally rooted in racism, white supremacy and national chauvinism that our military masters could probably have loaded that island sanctuary down with enemy combatants until it sank, with few serious political consequences. Various civil-libertarian legal organizations filed lawsuits about Guantanamo, but were off-handedly thrown out of court with that age-old excuse of bureaucrats everywhere, "lack of jurisdiction."

The contrast with the handling of [John Walker] Lindh's case [in which an American Muslim citizen was captured in Afghanistan fighting with the Taliban], the white guy from Marin [an affluent county in Northern California], couldn't have been more stark. He was thrown into the slammer, but the keys weren't thrown away. He got a lawyer (and a good one, at that), and was heading towards an honest-to-goodness trial before he cut a deal.

In July, 2002, Lindh accepted a plea bargain that included a provision that, if he ever engaged in "terrorist" activity again, he would be treated as an enemy combatant, and thus deprived of his normal "due process" constitutional rights. This may have been a good deal for Lindh, but it set a very dangerous precedent for future defendants, especially those not so well sheltered by affluent parents and high-powered attorneys.

And then along came Yaser Esam Hamdi.

Hamdi shook up the paradigm. No white guy he. But, born in Louisiana the same year that Ronald Reagan was elected President [1980], he was a U.S. citizen, despite the fact that his family later moved to Saudi Arabia. At some point he went off to Afghanistan, according to his father, to do relief work. He was eventually seized by the warlords of the Northern Alliance. The warlords turned him over to the U.S. military. The U.S. imprisoned him for a while in Afghanistan, then sent him to Guantanamo.

Later, learning that Hamdi was a U.S. citizen, they realized that they had a hot potato in hand. Holding a citizen as an enemy combatant in Guantanamo might cause problems for the "lack of jurisdiction" argument that had been keeping the civil-libertarian lawyers from making any headway in their Guantanamo lawsuits. So they shipped Hamdi stateside, to a naval brig in Norfolk, Virginia. Later still, they sent him to a brig in Charleston, South Carolina. This guy has been everywhere except Abu Ghraib [an American-run prison in Iraq that was the focus of a prisoner abuse scandal in 2004]. . . .

Inventing Enemy Combatant Laws

In mid-October [2004], over two months after the July Supreme Court rulings [in the cases concerning enemy combatants' rights] Hamdi was released from the brig he shared with [José] Padilla [another U.S. citizen held as an enemy combatant for his connection with a "dirty bomb" plot], and flown to Saudi Arabia, bereft of his U.S. citizenship, and with a whole slew of extraordinary conditions. The negotiations that led to this outcome began with the July ruling on his case.

The decision in the *Hamdi* case consists of four different written opinions. None alone commands a majority.

The ringleaders in the *Hamdi* decision, who signed the controlling opinion, are a subset of the Felonious Five [nickname for the five justices who ruled that Bush won the 2000 presidential election]—[William] Rehnquist, [Anthony] Kennedy and [Sandra Day] O'Connor. O'Connor wrote the decision. These three were joined by Stephen Breyer.

The key finding by this gang of four [a reference to the notorious Gang of Four who led Communist China's Cultural Revolution in the 1960s] is to uphold the concept of enemy combatants, for citizens and non-citizens alike. "There is no bar to this Nation's holding one of its own citizens as an enemy combatant," they boldly declare.

Having so blithely dispensed with the fundamental issue, the gang gets down to the work of defining what "due process" rights a person has once they have been declared an enemy combatant. Here they are venturing out into uncharted territory.

Since the whole concept of enemy combatants is make-believe to begin with, there are no laws or precedents on which they can rely. So they just make it up as they go along.

Innocent until proven guilty? Nope. "The Constitution would not be offended by a presumption in favor of the Government's evidence. . . . Thus, once the Government puts forth credible evidence that the habeas petitioner meets the enemy-combatant criteria, the onus could shift to the petitioner to rebut that evidence . . .

What kind of evidence can the government submit? Just about anything, apparently. According to the ruling, even hearsay is fine, as it "may need to be accepted as the most reliable available evidence . . ."

Right to an attorney? Sort of, sometimes, maybe. Hamdi's attorney argued that his client should have had the right to an attorney when he was first detained. But according to the gang of four, while Hamdi "has the right to access to counsel in connection with the proceedings on remand," since Hamdi now has an attorney, "no further consideration of this issue is necessary at this stage of the case." Punt that ball.

Trial by jury? Don't be silly. Be satisfied with "a meaningful opportunity to contest the factual basis for that detention before a neutral decisionmaker," whatever that means. Indeed, the ruling explicitly states that an "appropriately authorized and properly constituted military tribunal" would probably meet "the standards we have articulated."

Indefinite detention? The decision states that "indefinite detention for the purpose of interrogation is not authorized." But, "if the record establishes that United States troops are still involved in active combat in Afghanistan," Hamdi's detention is just fine, until whenever. Anybody taking guesses on when the "war on terror" in Afghanistan will be over?

Notably, these proposals for the evisceration of the Constitution and the Bill of Rights for enemy combatants are only an outline. In the words of the gang of four, "enemy combatant proceedings may be tailored to alleviate their uncommon potential to burden the Executive at a time of ongoing military conflict."

Now, put all this in the context of O'Connor's much-quoted statement that "We have long since made it clear that a state of war is not a blank check for the President when it comes to the rights of the Nation's citizens." This decision may not give the President a blank check, but if you win the lottery, you aren't going to complain too loudly about not getting a "blank check." . . .

The New Precedent for Exile

On October 11, [2004,] Hamdi was put on a plane and flown to Saudi Arabia, where he was greeted by his family. Hamdi's attorney had negotiated a deal that got Hamdi out of the brig, although with some draconian conditions. This undoubtedly felt like a victory to Hamdi, who might otherwise have spent many more years in confinement, facing a decidedly uncertain future.

But the conditions of his release, the precedent that it sets, and the issues in the Court's ruling left hanging, should give us all considerable pause.

Under the terms of his release, Hamdi was forced to:

- Renounce his U.S. citizenship.

- Pledge not to sue for his travails of the last three years.

- Promise not to leave Saudi Arabia for five years.

- Agree never to travel to Afghanistan, Iraq, Pakistan, Syria, Israel, the West Bank or Gaza.

- Advise the U.S. embassy 30 days before any foreign travel.

"I wanted to sign anything, everything, just to get out of there, to get back here," Hamdi told the press shortly after his release.

Under the circumstances, who wouldn't do what Hamdi did? As with Lindh's plea bargain, this was probably a good deal for the defendant. But it wasn't a very good deal for the Constitution and the Bill of Rights.

"For the first time in American history a citizen has been stripped of his citizenship and deported without ever having been charged with a crime," writes *CounterPunch* wag Mike Whitney. "The [Supreme] Court ... by refusing to force the government to either release Hamdi or charge him with a crime" paved the way for yet another weapon to be added to the arsenal of our post-9/11 rulers: "the threat of exile."

For those who might think that this deal was just an isolated instance of zealous prosecutors and a desperate detainee, consider that one of the key provisions in the Bush administration's proposed Patriot Act II would allow the government to revoke the citizenship of U.S. citizens, no matter how long their family has lived in the U.S.—and then deport that individual to god-only-knows-where.

Others Threatened as Enemy Combatants

Recall that "Marin Taliban" Lindh was forced, as part of his plea bargain, to consent to being designated an enemy combatant if he ever engaged in "terrorist" activity again.

Consider that Federal prosecutors reportedly used the threat of an enemy combatant designation during plea negotiations with the six Arab Americans from Lackawanna, New York, who were accused of being a "sleeper cell," forcing them into guilty pleas of providing material support to terrorists.

Think about Lyman Faris, a naturalized U.S. citizen from Kashmir, doing 20 years after pleading guilty to, among other things, casing out the Brooklyn Bridge to see if an al Qaeda squad could bring it down with cable cutters. Faris reportedly pled guilty after prosecutors discussed the idea of declaring him an enemy combatant. Faris reportedly tried to withdraw his guilty plea. His plea agreement is being held under seal, and officials refuse to say when and where he was arrested, or where he is currently being held.

If the designation of a U.S. citizen as an enemy combatant, or as a "terrorist," can lead to the revocation of citizenship and exile, perhaps even to some torture chamber in the dungeons of one of the empire's far-flung allies, what rights do we have left? . . .

New Types of Criminality

The "major victory" line on the enemy combatant Supreme Court rulings serves only to disorient the left and the public at large. No matter how bad it gets, there are those who insist on maintaining a certain official optimism whereby even defeat is transformed into victory. New categories of criminality like enemy combatants or domestic terrorists are invented and imposed on the body politic, but, not to worry, our progressive leaders have everything under control. Leave it to them.

But, today, Jose Padilla continues to languish in a navy brig. Yaser Esam Hamdi lives in exile in Saudi Arabia. Hundreds of prisoners in Guantanamo are still caught in a legal black hole. And many more rot away in secret detention facilities in countless untold places throughout the empire.

Ali Saleh Kahlab al-Marri, a citizen of Qatar, is locked away today in the same navy brig as Jose Padilla. Like Padilla, he was arrested in the U.S., while attending graduate school in Illinois. First, he was held as a "material witness." Then he was charged with making false statements. Finally, he was declared an enemy combatant. His attorneys filed a suit, but in early October [2004], the Supreme Court declined to consider his petition, because his attorneys allegedly filed his suit in the wrong court, just like Padilla's attorney. Al-Marri's lawyer claims that he was declared an enemy combatant because he refused to plead guilty. Al-Marri desperately needs a "major victory." . . .

We now have the construct of enemy combatants embedded, to use a modern term, into our legal and political system. That's bad news, anyway you cut it, no matter what your progressive lawyer friends tell you.

Chapter 3

Military Commissions
Violate the Law

Case Overview: *Hamdan v. Rumsfeld* (2006)

During the U.S. invasion of Afghanistan in October 2001, an Afghan militia unit supporting American ground troops captured Salim Ahmed Hamdan, a Yemeni national who once served as a driver for al Qaeda leader Osama bin Laden when Bin Laden was working on a civil project in that country. The militia turned Hamdan over to its U.S. allies who, in 2002, sent the captive to detention facilities at the Guantánamo Naval Base in Cuba. In that same year, the White House enacted Military Commission Order No. 1, which outlined the procedures to be used to try prisoners of the war on terror by military tribunal. In 2004 Hamdan was arraigned before a Combatant Status Review Tribunal (CSRT) and deemed an "enemy combatant" eligible to stand before a military commission. He was formally charged with conspiracy "to commit ... offenses triable by military commission."

Hamdan admitted he worked for bin Laden for many years, but he denied that he was anything more than a civilian driver. Unwilling to plead guilty to the charge, Hamdan authorized his military appointed defense counsel to challenge his detention in the federal court system. Hamdan's lawyers filed a petition for writ of habeas corpus, asserting that military commissions were not convened in accordance with the law and lacked the protections of a fair trial as guaranteed by the Geneva Conventions and the U.S. Uniform Code of Military Justice (UCMJ). One hour into Hamdan's federal trial in a U.S. District Court, Judge James Robertson agreed with the plaintiff's claims, averring that the government's CSRT had failed to prove that Hamdan was not a prisoner of war and therefore protected by the Geneva Conventions. Robertson also warned that the military commissions should be disbanded unless they conform to the UCMJ rule that such forums offer at least as many procedural protections as U.S. service personnel would receive in a common court-martial.

The government appealed the circuit court decision and won its case in the U.S. Court of Appeals for the District of Columbia. There, the three-judge panel affirmed that military commissions are legally constituted courts approved by Congress and are an appropriate venue for trying Hamdan. The appellate court also stated that Hamdan had no recourse to the Geneva Conventions because they are an international treaty among nations, and al Qaeda does not qualify as a nation. Based on these conclusions, the court of appeals reversed the lower court's decision.

In November 2005, Hamdan's lawyers petitioned the U.S. Supreme Court to review the appellate decision. When the Supreme Court agreed to hear the case, chief justice John Roberts recused himself because he had been one of the three judges ruling in the appellate case. The remaining eight judges heard testimony from both sides on March 28, 2006. The government asserted that the Supreme Court did not have jurisdiction in the matter under preclusions established by the Detainee Treatment Act of 2005, but the Court concluded differently. Delivering the Court's 5-3 verdict in favor of the plaintiff, Justice John Paul Stevens ignored the president's right to convene military commissions but contended that the commissions, as established, violated statutory law. Stevens inferred from *Ex parte Quirin*, a 1942 Supreme Court case involving the right to try Nazi saboteurs by military tribunal, that such commissions must abide by the rules of war. This, in the Court's opinion, meant complying with the protections afforded in the Geneva Conventions and the UCMJ, especially those rules that permit the accused to be present when evidence is introduced and the right to know all but the most sensitive evidence used in supporting the charge. The Court also concluded that the charge of "conspiracy" does not qualify as a violation triable by military commission.

The three dissenting judges all agreed with the initial government claim that the federal court system has no authority to hear the case and therefore should have dismissed it. This conclusion was strengthened in October 2006 when Congress passed the Military Commissions Act, which asserted that military commissions could be used to try those accused of violating the laws of war. The Military Commissions Act also stripped all courts of the authority to hear habeas corpus petitions from detainees or to "consider any other action against the United States or its agents relating to any aspect of the detention, transfer, treatment, trial, or conditions of confinement of an alien who is or was detained by the United States." This new law effectively invalidated Hamdan's arguments, and in May 2007 he was charged with conspiracy and providing support to terrorists. In two subsequent trials, these charges were dropped, however, and in December 2007, a military judge reviewed the case against Hamdan and determined that he was an "unlawful enemy combatant"—not a prisoner of war—and could stand trial by military commission. Hamdan's defense team continues to argue against this ruling.

> *"The procedures that the Government has decreed will govern Hamdan's trial by commission violate [domestic and international] laws."*

The Court's Decision: Military Commissions Contravene U.S. and International Law

John Paul Stevens

The petitioner in the U.S. Supreme Court case Hamdan v. Rumsfeld *argues that the president of the United States lacks the authority to try prisoners captured in the war on terror by specially created military commissions. In the following majority opinion of the Court, associate justice John Paul Stevens concurs with the petitioner's claim. Setting aside the question of whether the chief executive has the power to convene military commissions, Stevens maintains that the president's tribunal has failed to demonstrate that Hamdan's alleged crime is a violation of the rules of war or that some overriding military necessity demands trial by special commission. In addition, Stevens argues that the tribunal in this instance violates the Geneva Conventions—an international agreement that dictates protections to persons captured in wartime—because Hamdan's commission is not a "regularly constituted court" as defined by the conventions.*

John Paul Stevens was appointed to the Court in 1975 by President Gerald Ford. Though given his position by a Republican president, Stevens has often voted with the more liberal elements of the Court.

John Paul Stevens, majority opinion, *Salim Ahmed Hamdan, Petitioner v. Donald H. Rumsfeld, Secretary of Defense et al.*, June 29, 2006.

The Constitution makes the President the "Commander in Chief" of the Armed Forces, Art. II, §2, but vests in Congress the powers to "declare War . . . and make Rules concerning Captures on Land and Water," to "raise and support Armies," to "define and punish . . . Offences against the Law of Nations," and "To make Rules for the Government and Regulation of the land and naval Forces." The interplay between these powers was described by Chief Justice [Solomon P.] Chase in the seminal case *Ex parte Milligan* [1866]:

> The power to make the necessary laws is in Congress; the power to execute in the President. Both powers imply many subordinate and auxiliary powers. Each includes all authorities essential to its due exercise. But neither can the President, in war more than in peace, intrude upon the proper authority of Congress, nor Congress upon the proper authority of the President. . . . Congress cannot direct the conduct of campaigns, nor can the President, or any commander under him, without the sanction of Congress, institute tribunals for the trial and punishment of offences, either of soldiers or civilians, unless in cases of a controlling necessity, which justifies what it compels, or at least insures acts of indemnity from the justice of the legislature.

Whether Chief Justice Chase was correct in suggesting that the President may constitutionally convene military commissions "without the sanction of Congress" in cases of "controlling necessity" is a question this Court has not answered definitively, and need not answer today. For we held in [*Ex Parte*] *Quirin* [1942] that Congress had, through Article of War 15, sanctioned the use of military commissions in such circumstances. ("By the Articles of War, and especially Article 15, Congress has explicitly provided, so far as it may constitutionally do so, that military tribunals shall have jurisdiction to try offenders or offenses against the law of war in appropriate cases"). Article 21 of the UCMJ [Uniform Code of Military

Justice], the language of which is substantially identical to the old Article 15 and was preserved by Congress after World War II, reads as follows:

> Jurisdiction of courts-martial not exclusive.
>
> The provisions of this code conferring jurisdiction upon courts-martial shall not be construed as depriving military commissions, provost courts, or other military tribunals of concurrent jurisdiction in respect of offenders or offenses that by statute or by the law of war may be tried by such military commissions, provost courts, or other military tribunals.

We have no occasion to revisit *Quirin's* controversial characterization of Article of War 15 as congressional authorization for military commissions. Contrary to the Government's assertion, however, even *Quirin* did not view the authorization as a sweeping mandate for the President to "invoke military commissions when he deems them necessary." Rather, the *Quirin* Court recognized that Congress had simply preserved what power, under the Constitution and the common law of war, the President had had before 1916 to convene military commissions—with the express condition that the President and those under his command comply with the law of war. . . .

No Authority to Convene Commissions

The Government would have us dispense with the inquiry that the *Quirin* Court undertook and find in either the AUMF [Authorization for Use of Military Force, 2001] or the DTA [Detainee Treatment Act of 2005] specific, overriding authorization for the very commission that has been convened to try Hamdan. Neither of these congressional Acts, however, expands the President's authority to convene military commissions. First, while we assume that the AUMF activated the President's war powers and that those powers include the authority to convene military commissions in appropriate circumstances, there is nothing in the text or legislative history of the AUMF even hinting that Congress intended to expand or alter the authorization set forth in Article 21 of the UCMJ. . . .

Likewise, the DTA cannot be read to authorize this commission. Although the DTA, unlike either Article 21 or the AUMF, was enacted after the President had convened Hamdan's commission, it contains no language authorizing that tribunal or any other at Guantanamo Bay. The DTA obviously "recognize[s]" the existence of the Guantanamo Bay commissions in the weakest sense because it references some of the military orders governing them and creates limited judicial review of their "final decision[s]." But the statute also pointedly reserves judgment on whether "the Constitution and laws of the United States are applicable" in reviewing such decisions and whether, if they are, the "standards and procedures" used to try Hamdan and other detainees actually violate the "Constitution and laws."

Together, the UCMJ, the AUMF, and the DTA at most acknowledge a general Presidential authority to convene military commissions in circumstances where justified under the "Constitution and laws," including the law of war. Absent a more specific congressional authorization, the task of this Court is, as it was in *Quirin*, to decide whether Hamdan's military commission is so justified. It is to that inquiry we now turn.

Appropriately Convened Commissions

The common law governing military commissions may be gleaned from past practice and what sparse legal precedent exists. Commissions historically have been used in three situations. . . . First, they have substituted for civilian courts at times and in places where martial law has been declared. Their use in these circumstances has raised constitutional questions, . . . but is well recognized. Second, commissions have been established to try civilians "as part of a temporary military government over occupied enemy territory regained from an enemy where civilian government cannot and does not function." . . . Illustrative of this second kind of commission is the one that was established, with jurisdiction to apply the German Criminal Code, in occupied Germany following the end of World War II. . . .

The third type of commission, convened as an "incident to the conduct of war" when there is a need "to seize and subject to disciplinary measures those enemies who in their attempt to thwart or impede our military effort have violated the law of war," *Quirin* 317 U.S., at 28–29, has been described as "utterly different" from the other two. . . . Not only is its jurisdiction limited to offenses cognizable during time of war, but its role is primarily a factfinding one—to determine, typically on the battlefield itself, whether the defendant has violated the law of war. The last time the U.S. Armed Forces used the law-of-war military commission was during World War II. In *Quirin*, this Court sanctioned President [Franklin D.] Roosevelt's use of such a tribunal to try Nazi saboteurs captured on American soil during the War. And in *Yamashita* [*v. Skyer*, 1946], we held that a military commission had jurisdiction to try a Japanese commander for failing to prevent troops under his command from committing atrocities in the Philippines.

Quirin is the model the Government invokes most frequently to defend the commission convened to try Hamdan. That is both appropriate and unsurprising. Since Guantanamo Bay is neither enemy-occupied territory nor under martial law, the law-of-war commission is the only model available. At the same time, no more robust model of executive power exists; *Quirin* represents the high-water mark of military power to try enemy combatants for war crimes.

The classic treatise penned by Colonel William Winthrop, whom we have called "the '[William] Blackstone of Military Law,'" *Reid v. Covert.* (1957) (plurality opinion), describes at least four preconditions for exercise of jurisdiction by a tribunal of the type convened to try Hamdan. First, "[a] military commission, (except where otherwise authorized by statute), can legally assume jurisdiction only of offenses committed within the field of the command of the convening commander." The "field of command" in these circumstances means the "theatre of war." Second, the offense charged "must have been committed within the period of the war." No jurisdiction exists to try offenses "committed either before or after the war." Third, a military commission not established pursuant to martial law or an occupation may try only "[i]ndividuals of the enemy's army who have been guilty of illegitimate warfare or other offences in violation of the laws of war" and members of one's own army "who, in time of war, become chargeable with crimes or offences not cognizable, or triable, by the criminal courts or under the Articles of war." Finally, a law-of-war commission has jurisdiction to try only two kinds of offense: "Violations of the laws and usages of war cognizable by military tribunals only," and "[b]reaches of military orders or regulations for which offenders are not legally triable by court-martial under the Articles of war."

All parties agree that Colonel Winthrop's treatise accurately describes the common law governing military commissions, and that the jurisdictional limitations he identifies were incorporated in Article of War 15 and, later, Article 21 of the UCMJ. It also is undisputed that Hamdan's commission lacks jurisdiction to try him unless the charge "properly set[s] forth, not only the details of the act charged, but the circumstances conferring *jurisdiction*." The question is whether the preconditions designed to ensure that a military necessity exists to justify the use of this extraordinary tribunal have been satisfied here.

Conspiracy Is Not a Recognized War Crime

The charge against Hamdan . . . alleges a conspiracy extending over a number of years, from 1996 to November 2001. All but two months of that more than 5-year-long period preceded the attacks of September 11, 2001, and the enactment of the AUMF—the Act of Congress on which the Government relies for exercise of its war powers and thus for its authority to convene military commissions. Neither the purported agreement with [al Qaeda leader] Osama bin Laden and others to commit war crimes, nor a single overt act, is alleged to have occurred in a theater of war or on any specified date after September 11, 2001. None of the overt acts that Hamdan is alleged to have committed violates the law of war.

These facts alone cast doubt on the legality of the charge and, hence, the commission; as Winthrop makes plain, the offense alleged must have been committed both in a theater of war and *during*, not before, the relevant conflict. But the deficiencies in the time and place allegations also underscore— indeed are symptomatic of—the most serious defect of this charge: The offense it alleges is not triable by law-of-war military commission. . . .

There is no suggestion that Congress has, in exercise of its constitutional authority to "define and punish . . . Offences against the Law of Nations," U.S. Const., positively identified "conspiracy" as a war crime. As we explained in *Quirin*, that is not necessarily fatal to the Government's claim of authority to try the alleged offense by military commission; Congress, through Article 21 of the UCMJ, has "incorporated by reference" the common law of war, which may render triable by military commission certain offenses not defined by statute. When, however, neither the elements of the offense nor the range of permissible punishments is defined by statute or treaty, the precedent must be plain and unambiguous. To demand any less would be to risk concentrating in military hands a degree of adjudicative and punitive power in excess of that contemplated either by statute or by the Constitution. . . .

This high standard was met in *Quirin*; the violation there alleged was, by "universal agreement and practice" both in this country and internationally, recognized as an offense against the law of war. . . . Although the picture arguably was less clear in *Yamashita*, . . . the disagreement between the majority and the dissenters in that case concerned whether the historic and textual evidence constituted clear precedent—not whether clear precedent was required to justify trial by law-of-war military commission.

At a minimum, the Government must make a substantial showing that the crime for which it seeks to try a defendant by military commission is acknowledged to be an offense against the law of war. That burden is far from satisfied here. The crime of "conspiracy" has rarely if ever been tried as such in this country by any law-of-war military commission not exercising some other form of jurisdiction, and does not appear in either the Geneva Conventions or the Hague Conventions—the major treaties on the law of war. Winthrop explains that under the common law governing military commissions, it is not enough to intend to violate the law of war and commit overt acts in furtherance of that intention unless the overt acts either are themselves offenses against the law of war or constitute steps sufficiently substantial to qualify as an attempt. . . .

Finally, international sources confirm that the crime charged here is not a recognized violation of the law of war. . . . None of the major treaties governing the law of war identifies conspiracy as a violation thereof. And the only "conspiracy" crimes that have been recognized by international war crimes tribunals (whose jurisdiction often extends beyond war crimes proper to crimes against humanity and crimes against the peace) are conspiracy to commit genocide and common plan to wage aggressive war, which is a crime against the peace and requires for its commission actual participation in a "concrete plan to wage war." . . .

No Necessity for Trial by Commission

The charge's shortcomings are not merely formal, but are indicative of a broader inability on the Executive's part here to satisfy the most basic precondition—at least in the absence of specific congressional authorization—for establishment of military commissions: military necessity. Hamdan's tribunal was appointed not by a military commander in the field of battle, but by a retired major general stationed away from any active hostilities. . . . Hamdan is charged not with an overt act for which he was caught redhanded in a theater of war and which military efficiency demands be tried expeditiously, but with an *agreement* the inception of which long predated the attacks of September 11, 2001 and the AUMF. That may well be a crime, but it is not an offense that "by the law of war may be tried by military commissio[n]." None of the overt acts alleged to have been committed in furtherance of the agreement is itself a war crime, or even necessarily occurred during time of, or in a theater of, war. Any urgent need for imposition or execution of judgment is utterly belied by the record; Hamdan was arrested in November 2001 and he was not charged until mid-2004. These simply are not the circumstances in which, by any stretch of the historical evidence or this Court's precedents, a military commission established by Executive Order under the authority of Article 21 of the UCMJ may lawfully try a person and subject him to punishment.

Whether or not the Government has charged Hamdan with an offense against the law of war cognizable by military commission, the commission lacks power to proceed. The UCMJ conditions the President's use of military commissions on compliance not only with the American common law of war, but also with the rest of the UCMJ itself, insofar as applicable, and with the "rules and precepts of the law of nations," *Quirin,*—including, *inter alia* [among other things], the four Geneva Conventions signed in 1949. The procedures that the Government has decreed will govern Hamdan's trial by commission violate these laws. . . .

Violating the Geneva Conventions

The procedures adopted to try Hamdan also violate the Geneva Conventions. The Court of Appeals [that first rendered judgment against Hamdan] dismissed Hamdan's Geneva Convention challenge. . . .

The Court of Appeals concluded that the Conventions did not . . . apply to the armed conflict during which Hamdan was captured. The court accepted the Executive's assertions that Hamdan was captured in connection with the United States' war with al Qaeda and that that war is distinct from the war with the Taliban in Afghanistan. It further reasoned that the war with al Qaeda evades the reach of the Geneva Conventions. . . . We . . . disagree with the latter conclusion.

The conflict with al Qaeda is not, according to the Government, a conflict to which the full protections afforded detainees under the 1949 Geneva Conventions apply because Article 2 of those Conventions (which appears in all four Conventions) renders the full protections applicable only to "all cases of declared war or of any other armed conflict which may arise between two or more of the High Contracting Parties." Since Hamdan was captured and detained incident to the conflict with al Qaeda and not the conflict with the Taliban, and since al Qaeda, unlike Afghanistan, is not a "High Contracting Party"—*i.e.*, a signatory of the Conventions, the protections of those Conventions are not, it is argued, applicable to Hamdan.

Article 3 Affords Minimal Protections

We need not decide the merits of this argument because there is at least one provision of the Geneva Conventions that applies here even if the relevant conflict is not one between signatories. Article 3, often referred to as Common Article 3 because, like Article 2, it appears in all four Geneva Conventions, provides that in a "conflict not of an international character occurring in the territory of one of the High Contracting Parties, each Party to the conflict shall be bound to apply, as a minimum," certain provisions protecting "[p]ersons taking no active part in the hostilities, including members of armed forces who have laid down their arms and those placed *hors de combat* [out of the fighting] by . . . detention." One such provision prohibits "the passing of sentences and the carrying out of executions without previous judgment pronounced by a regularly constituted court affording all the judicial guarantees which are recognized as indispensable by civilized peoples."

The Court of Appeals thought, and the Government asserts, that Common Article 3 does not apply to Hamdan because the conflict with al Qaeda, being "'international in scope,'" does not qualify as a "'conflict not of an international character.'" That reasoning is erroneous. The term "conflict not of an international character" is used here in contradistinction to a conflict between nations. So much is demonstrated by the "fundamental logic [of] the Convention's provisions on its application." Common Article 2 provides that "the present Convention shall apply to all cases of declared war or of any other armed conflict which may arise between two or more of the High Contracting Parties." High Contracting Parties (signatories) also must abide by all terms of the Conventions vis-à-vis one another even if one party to the conflict is a nonsignatory "Power," and must so abide vis-à-vis the nonsignatory if "the latter accepts and applies" those terms. Common Article 3, by contrast, affords some minimal protection, falling short of full protection under the Conventions, to individuals associated with neither a signatory nor even a nonsignatory "Power" who are involved in a conflict "in the territory of" a signatory. The latter kind of conflict is distinguishable from the conflict described in Common Article 2 chiefly because it does not involve a clash between nations (whether signatories or not). In context, then the phrase "not of an International character" bears its literal meaning. . . .

Although the official commentaries accompanying Common Article 3 indicate that an important purpose of the provision was to furnish minimal protection to rebels involved in one kind of "conflict not of an international character," *i.e.*, a civil war, the commentaries also make clear "that the scope of the Article must be as wide as possible." In fact, limiting language that would have rendered Common Article 3 applicable "especially [to] cases of civil war, colonial conflicts, or wars of religion," was omitted from the final version of the Article, which coupled broader scope of application with a narrower range of rights than did earlier proposed iterations.

Common Article 3, then, is applicable here and, as indicated above, requires that Hamdan be tried by a "regularly constituted court affording all the judicial guarantees which are recognized as indispensable by civilized peoples." While the term "regularly constituted court" is not specifically defined in either Common Article 3 or its accompanying commentary, other sources disclose its core meaning. The commentary accompanying a provision of the Fourth Geneva Convention, for example, defines "'regularly constituted'" tribunals to include "ordinary military courts" and "definitely exclud[e] all special tribunals." . . .

As Justice [Anthony] Kennedy explains, that defense fails because "[t]he regular military courts in our system are the courts-martial established by congressional statutes." . . .

We agree with Justice Kennedy that the procedures adopted to try Hamdan deviate from those governing courts-martial in ways not justified by any "evident practical need," and for that reason, at least, fail to afford the requisite guarantees.

"There is no reason why a court that differs in structure or composition from an ordinary military court must be viewed as having been improperly constituted."

Dissenting Opinion: Military Commissions Are Regularly Constituted Courts

Samuel Alito Jr.

In the case of Hamdan v. Rumsfeld, *the U.S. Supreme Court ruled five to three that the executive branch of government lacks the authority to convene military commissions because, in part, these tribunals are not "regularly constituted" courts as indicated by international law. In his dissenting opinion, Justice Samuel Alito Jr. argues that because no international law defines how courts should be established, each nation must look to its own domestic laws for guidance and sanction. According to Alito, the United States has often set up nontraditional courts to try criminals, and none have been deemed irregular. Alito also asserts that military commissions cannot be termed invalid merely because of supposed procedural problems. The "appropriate remedy" in that case, he maintains, "is to proscribe the use of those particular procedures, not outlaw the commissions."*

Appointed to the U.S. Supreme Court by President George W. Bush in 2005, Samuel Alito Jr. has often tendered opinions that favor conservative rulings of the Court. Prior to this appointment, Alito served as a U.S. attorney for the District of

Samuel Alito Jr., dissenting opinion, *Salim Ahmed Hamdan, Petitioner v. Donald H. Rumsfeld, Secretary of Defense et al.*, June 29, 2006.

New Jersey (1977–1981) and was a judge on the United States Court of Appeals for the Third Circuit (1990–2006).

The holding of the Court, as I understand it, rests on the following reasoning. A military commission is lawful only if it is authorized by 10 U.S.C. §821 [part of the Uniform Code of Military Justice]; this provision permits the use of a commission to try "offenders or offenses" that "by statute or by the law of war may be tried by" such a commission; because no statute provides that an offender such as petitioner [Hamdan] or an offense such as the one with which he is charged may be tried by a military commission, he may be tried by military commission only if the trial is authorized by "the law of war"; the Geneva Conventions are part of the law of war; and Common Article 3 of the Conventions prohibits petitioner's trial because the commission before which he would be tried is not "a regularly constituted court" ... I disagree with this holding because petitioner's commission is "a regularly constituted court."

Common Article 3 provides as follows:

In the case of armed conflict not of an international character occurring in the territory of one of the High Contracting Parties, each Party to the conflict shall be bound to apply, as a minimum, the following provisions:

(1)...[T]he following acts are and shall remain prohibited ...:

(d) The passing of sentences and the carrying out of executions without previous judgment pronounced by *a regularly constituted court* affording all the judicial guarantees which are recognized as indispensable by civilized peoples. (emphasis added).

Common Article 3 thus imposes three requirements. Sentences may be imposed only by (1) a "court" (2) that is "regularly constituted" and (3) that affords "all the judicial guarantees which are recognized as indispensable by civilized peoples."

Standards for Regularly Constituted Courts

I see no need here to comment extensively on the meaning of the first and third requirements. The first requirement is largely self-explanatory, and, with respect to the third, I note only that on its face it imposes a uniform international standard that does not vary from signatory to signatory.

The second element ("regularly constituted") is the one on which the Court relies, and I interpret this element to require that the court be appointed or established in accordance with the appointing country's domestic law. I agree with the Court that, as used in Common Article 3, the term "regularly" is synonymous with "properly." The term "constitute" means "appoint," "set up," or "establish," *Webster's Third New International Dictionary* 486 (1961), and therefore "regularly constituted" means properly appointed, set up, or established. Our cases repeatedly use the phrases "regularly constituted" and "properly constituted" in this sense.

In order to determine whether a court has been properly appointed, set up, or established, it is necessary to refer to a body of law that governs such matters. I interpret Common Article 3 as looking to the domestic law of the appointing country because I am not aware of any international law standard regarding the way in which such a court must be appointed, set up, or established, and because different countries with different government structures handle this matter differently. Accordingly, "a regularly constituted court" is a court that has been appointed, set up, or established in accordance with the domestic law of the appointing country.

Military Commissions Regularly Constituted

In contrast to this interpretation, the opinions supporting the judgment today hold that the military commission before which petitioner would be tried is not "a regularly constituted court" (a) because "no evident practical need explains" why its "structure and composition ... deviate from conventional court-martial standards," and (b) because, contrary to 10 U. S. C. §836(b), the procedures specified for use in the proceeding before the military commission impermissibly differ from those provided under the Uniform Code of Military Justice (UCMJ) for use by courts-martial I do not believe that either of these grounds is sound.

I see no basis for the Court's holding that a military commission cannot be regarded as "a regularly constituted court" unless it is similar in structure and composition to a regular military court or unless there is an "evident practical need" for the divergence. There is no reason why a court that differs in structure or composition from an ordinary military court must be viewed as having been improperly constituted. Tribunals that vary significantly in structure, composition, and procedures may all be "regularly" or "properly" constituted. Consider, for example, a municipal court, a state trial court of general jurisdiction, an Article I federal trial court, a federal district court, and an international court, such as the International Criminal Tribunal for the Former Yugoslavia. Although these courts are "differently constituted" and differ substantially in many other respects, they are all "regularly constituted."

If Common Article 3 had been meant to require trial before a country's military courts or courts that are similar in structure and composition, the drafters almost certainly would have used language that expresses that thought more directly. Other provisions of the Convention Relative to the Treatment of Prisoners of War refer expressly to the ordinary military courts and expressly prescribe the "uniformity principle" that Justice [Anthony] Kennedy sees in Common Article 3. ... Article 84 provides that "[a] prisoner of war shall be tried only by a military court, unless the existing laws of the Detaining

Power expressly permit the civil courts to try a member of the armed forces of the Detaining Power in respect of the particular offence alleged to have been committed by the prisoner of war." Article 87 states that "prisoners of war may not be sentenced by the military authorities and courts of the Detaining Power to any penalties except those provided for in respect of members of the armed forces of the said Power who have committed the same acts." Similarly, Article 66 of the Geneva Convention Relative to the Treatment of Civilian Persons in Time of War—a provision to which the Court looks for guidance in interpreting Common Article 3—expressly provides that civilians charged with committing crimes in occupied territory may be handed over by the occupying power "to its properly constituted, non-political military courts, on condition that the said courts sit in the occupied country." If Common Article 3 had been meant to incorporate a "uniformity principle," it presumably would have used language like that employed in the provisions noted above. For these reasons, I cannot agree with the Court's conclusion that the military commission at issue here is not a "regularly constituted court" because its structure and composition differ from those of a court-martial.

No Conflict with Military Commissions

Contrary to the suggestion of the Court, . . . the commentary on Article 66 of the Fourth Geneva Convention does not undermine this conclusion. As noted, Article 66 permits an occupying power to try civilians in its "properly constituted, non-political military courts." The commentary on this provision states:

> The courts are to be 'regularly constituted'. This wording definitely excludes all special tribunals. It is the ordinary military courts of the Occupying Power which will be competent.

The Court states that this commentary "defines 'regularly constituted' tribunals to include 'ordinary military courts' and 'definitely exclud[e] all special tribunals.'" ... This much is clear from the commentary itself. Yet the mere statement that a military court *is* a regularly constituted tribunal is of no help in addressing petitioner's claim that his commission *is not* such a tribunal. As for the commentary's mention of "special tribunals," it is doubtful whether we should take this gloss on Article 66—which forbids an *occupying power* from trying *civilians* in courts set up specially for that purpose—to tell us much about the very different context addressed by Common Article 3.

But even if Common Article 3 recognizes this prohibition on "special tribunals," that prohibition does not cover petitioner's tribunal. If "special" means anything in contradistinction to "regular," it would be in the sense of "special" as "relating to a single thing," and "regular" as "uniform in course, practice, or occurrence." *Webster's Third New International Dictionary* 2186, 1913. Insofar as respondents propose to conduct the tribunals according to the procedures of Military Commission Order No. 1 and orders promulgated thereunder—and nobody has suggested respondents intend otherwise—then it seems that petitioner's tribunal, like the hundreds of others respondents propose to conduct, is very much regular and not at all special.

Not the Remedy for Procedural Problems

I also disagree with the Court's conclusion that petitioner's military commission is "illegal," ... because its procedures allegedly do not comply with 10 U. S. C. §836. Even if §836(b), unlike Common Article 3, does impose at least a limited uniformity requirement amongst the tribunals contemplated by the UCMJ, and even if it is assumed for the sake of argument that some of the procedures specified in Military Commission Order No. 1 impermissibly deviate from court-martial procedures, it does not follow that the military commissions created by that order are not "regularly constituted" or that trying petitioner before such a commission would be inconsistent with the law of war. If Congress enacted a statute requiring the federal district courts to follow a procedure that is unconstitutional, the statute would be invalid, but the district courts would not. Likewise, if some of the procedures that may be used in military commission proceedings are improper, the appropriate remedy is to proscribe the use of those particular procedures, not to outlaw the commissions. I see no justification for striking down the entire commission structure simply because it is possible that petitioner's trial might involve the use of some procedure that is improper.

> *"The whole point of this ruling in Hamdan [was] to move the president from violating the law to complying with [it]."*

The President Must Comply with Law

Walter Dellinger and Dahlia Lithwick

Walter Dellinger is a practicing lawyer and a professor of law at Duke University. He has served as the acting United States solicitor general (1996–1997) and as assistant attorney general and head of the Office of Legal Counsel from 1993 to 1996. In the following viewpoint, Dellinger states that the importance of the U.S. Supreme Court case Hamdan v. Rumsfeld *has little to do with the legality of military commissions used to try suspected terrorists. Instead, to Dellinger, the Court's judgment is significant because it reins in executive power. According to Dellinger, President George W. Bush's establishment of military commissions was not sanctioned by Congress and has no basis in the Constitution. The Court's* Hamdan *ruling, therefore, affirmed that the president cannot operate above the law.*

Dear Dahlia...

You are right that opinions are mixed on how significant [June 29, 2006's] *Hamdan* decision is. Views seem to range from a ho-hum from the usually very astute Richard Samp of the Washington Legal Foundation (he'd "be surprised if any of the holdings ... end up having large practical significance") all the way to . . . well, I guess all the way to *me*. My flash assessment that it was "the most important decision on presidential power ever" seems to have come in as yesterday's high bid. Having had a night to sleep on *Hamdan*, listen to others' reactions, and read the morning papers, I guess I should reconsider the "importance" question.

Well, one might ask, what presidential power decision is there that exceeds *Hamdan* in importance? Quite possibly *U.S. v. Nixon*, the decision that required the president to hand over tape recordings that turned him prematurely into an ex-president. Another candidate is, of course, *Youngstown Sheet & Tube v. Sawyer* . . . (1952), the landmark case in which the court ordered President [Harry] Truman to return the steel mills he had seized to avert a strike during the Korean War; *Youngstown* set the standard for assessing claims of unilateral presidential power. Each of those cases, however, was still something of a "one-off." Nixon knew he was breaking the law and hoped not to get caught; Truman thought the steel strike was a special case and did not otherwise act as if he could disregard Congress.

Rejecting Imperial Claim

In *Hamdan*, however, the court confronted and rejected a deep theory of the Constitution that had been developed by the incumbent administration and was invoked to justify perhaps hundreds of executive decisions (so many of which seem to be secret we will never even know how many) that at least appeared to violate valid acts of Congress. The rejection of that imperial claim is what is important about this case.

It's not about the military commissions. I think what explains differing assessments of the importance of *Hamdan* is that different people are all viewing the decision from different levels of generality. And the farther back you stand, the more significant it appears. Up close, it's a case about Mr. Hamdan, or maybe about Hamdan and a dozen others.

Whether it makes much difference to them is hard to say. If you look at it as a case about the validity of shortcut military commissions, it looks a bit more significant, but Congress will provide some kind of fix for those commissions.

But that is not what *Hamdan* is really about. As Marty Lederman of Georgetown Law Center said to me, future historians are about as likely to think of *Hamdan* as a "military commissions case" as they are to think of *Youngstown Sheet & Steel v. Sawyer* as a decision about "steel mill law." *Hamdan* is about the OLC [Office of Legal Counsel] torture memo; and it's about whether the president can refuse to comply with the McCain Amendment.[1] It's about all those laws the president says, as he signs them, that he will not commit to obey, if in his view foreign relations or deliberative processes of the executive or other matters may be affected. And, by the way, he won't even commit to tell Congress he is not obeying the law. That is what it's about.

Presidential Power Can Be Limited

It's been really frustrating to me that so many people—including critics of the president—fail to understand what's at the essence of the fundamental constitutional claim of this administration. Even such an incisive critic of presidential overreaching as Senate Judiciary Chair Arlen Specter puts the issue in a confusing way. At Hearings on Signing Statements at the beginning of *Hamdan* he made the concession that, "There is no doubt that the president's constitutional power under Article II cannot be limited by statute."

But almost all—not all, but almost all—of what presidents do in the exercise of their Article II powers certainly *can* be limited by statute. Certainly, no act of Congress is necessary to enable the president as commander in chief to discipline and

1. The OLC torture memo was written in 2002 and directed to White House attorneys. It cited legal definitions of what was not considered torture in the interrogation of prisoners. The McCain Amendment prohibits inhumane treatment of detainees at Guantánamo Bay and later became the Detainee Treatment Act of 2005.

punish members of the armed forces. That is surely a "constitutional power under Article II," but it just as surely can be "limited by statute." And it has been for over 200 years with enactments such as the Uniform Code of Military Justice—laws never seriously thought to be unconstitutional.

There are actually only a very few core executive functions that Congress may not touch. But where . . . Congress has its own legislative authority, the president has to show how those core functions of his would be jeopardized by complying with the law. And as the court noted, no such showing was even seriously attempted in *Hamdan*.

The Executive Must Comply with the Law

The White House's response to *Hamdan* was to shrug that it "requires little more than having Congress put its stamp of approval" on the modified military trial plans or maybe on the existing plan. But that is the whole point of this ruling in *Hamdan*—to move the president from violating the law to complying with a new law to be enacted by Congress.

A short while back, there seemed to be no stopping the sweeping and untenable assertions of a presidential power to disregard laws that seemed entirely constitutional to me. I had thought we had effectively lost the principle that the president—indeed, the whole executive branch of government—was really required to comply with valid federal laws constitutionally enacted by Congress. Now I think that principle has been not merely affirmed but also re-enshrined. How many cases can be more important than that?

Hamdan Reveals America's Commitment to the Geneva Conventions

Aziz Huq

Aziz Huq directs the Liberty and National Security Project at the Brennan Center for Justice, a part of the New York University Law School that does litigation on presidential detention and policy work on presidential power and congressional oversight. In the following assessment of the case, Huq discredits those critics who believe that the Geneva Conventions—an international agreement that dictates protections to persons captured in wartime—give terrorists too many rights given that they commonly do not abide by the rules of war. Huq asserts that the Geneva Conventions do not afford equal protections to terrorists and lawful combatants, and they do not exempt terrorists from trial and punishment for their part in conflicts. However, as Huq states, they do provide a minimum of humane treatment to anyone captured in battle, and maintaining such standards will help America ensure that its credibility does not suffer in the important ideological struggle against those who defame America and its values.

The Supreme Court's ruling [on June 29, 2006,] in *Hamdan* that military commissions erected at Guantánamo are inconsistent with our military law and the Geneva Conven-

Aziz Huq, "What Geneva Means to *Hamdan*," *TomPaine.com*, July 7, 2006. Reproduced by permission.

tions has already prompted fierce—and flawed—debate. One key question, especially relevant in [the subsequent] Judiciary Committee hearings on *Hamdan*, is whether and how the Geneva Conventions apply to military commissions. The many factually and legally incorrect assertions clogging the air make it worth stepping back to understand what Geneva does, and why it matters for our success against the terrorist threat.

Overheated rhetoric on Geneva began within hours of the court's decision. Summing up the criticism, the *Wall Street Journal* argued that it was deeply improper to give terrorist suspects the same rights as American servicemen. The *Journal* contended that prosecutions of suspected terrorists would compromise the president's ability to act with "speed and decisiveness." These criticisms rest, however, on misconceptions about Geneva and ignorance about the workings of our military justice system.

The Reach of the Geneva Conventions

The United States and other nations negotiated the Geneva Conventions in August 1949, as World War II's aftermath smoldered around them. America's negotiators, Raymond Yingling and Robert Ginnane, had a clear mission: To secure clear rules placing out of bounds the kind of abuse and torture American soldiers captured by Japan had suffered. The negotiators must have known of the Ofuma interrogation center, where American soldiers were subjected to solitary confinement, blindfolding and stress positions such as the "Ofuma crunch": an excruciatingly painful position that involves "standing on the ball of your foot, knees half bent and arms extended over the head." The four Conventions thus contain literally hundreds of detailed provisions, not only preventing this kind of abuse, but also reaching food rationing, barracks arrangements, and even sports.

Geneva's intricate rules, however, govern only the treatment of persons who are no longer fighting, and only in times of armed conflict. They say nothing about combat decisions: weapons used, tactics employed and strategic goals selected. Geneva focuses solely on those "hors de combat" [matters outside of combat] The wounded, captured and civilians; the shepherd who inadvertently strayed onto the battlefield. Geneva imposes no constraint on the military's use of force, or its "speed and decisiveness," as the *Journal* misleadingly suggested. It kicks in only once the fetters are securely fastened on prisoners.

Further, President Harry S. Truman signed, and the Senate ratified, the Geneva treaties knowing full well that they applied only in "armed conflicts" (including both conflicts between two states and conflicts involving only one state). The White House and the Congress entered into the treaties—and even made "grave breaches" of Geneva violations of American criminal law—knowing full well that Geneva's restrictions applied only when American servicemen's lives were at stake. Every time Geneva kicks in, it is because American soldiers are in the line of fire. Equally, every time American soldiers walk into battle, they know that an intricate and detailed web of legal protections shield them from abuse and ill-treatment.

Separate Protections

But didn't the Supreme Court hold that these detailed rules about sports and food rationing apply to alleged al-Qaida and Taliban members as well as to U.S. forces? Isn't the *Journal* correct to say that American soldiers and alleged al-Qaida members captured on the Afghan battlefield are being equally ranked? Absolutely not. A captured American soldier and an alleged al-Qaida member picked up during combat are almost certainly subject to different rules and protections, and the Court's ruling did not change that. It is the *Journal*'s failure to understand Geneva that fosters confusion.

Geneva protects the American soldier in two ways. First, he is entitled to "combatant immunity." That is, he cannot be tried for his acts as a soldier, carrying and using a gun, killing others. Second, because he is a "lawful combatant" under Geneva, he benefits from more than one hundred detailed rules for the treatment of "Prisoners of War," or POWs, that are listed in the Third Geneva Convention. These are the rules on food rations, barracks arrangements, and sports Yingling and Ginnane negotiated in 1949.

But the al-Qaida fighter likely gets neither benefit if he has not followed Geneva's demanding rules for POW entitlement. If the al-Qaida member fails to meet these rules—and there's a reasonable argument many of them did fail—they do not rank as POWs, and do not obtain the benefits of that status, including combatant immunity. The al-Qaida fighter, in other words, can be tried and convicted criminally as a result of his failure to follow the laws of war. Unlike the American service member, the al-Qaida fighter is not a "lawful" combatant under Geneva.

Minimum Guarantees of Article 3

But Geneva is a comprehensive framework for everyone captured in warfare. Hence, it has a minimal baseline standard for any person captured during wartime, a baseline that precludes "[o]utrages upon personal dignity, in particular, humiliating and degrading treatment," and also criminal trials outside of a "regularly constituted court affording all the judicial guarantees which are recognized as indispensable by civilized peoples." This is "Common Article 3."

"Common Article 3"—called because it appears in each of the four Conventions—is the point beyond which no nation can go without losing its claim to dignity and honor. Geneva's drafters (including the United States), President [Harry] Truman, and the U.S. Senate concluded that the limit on torture and unfair trials formed such bare essentials.

It is solely Common Article 3 that was at issue in *Hamdan*. It was solely this irreducible floor that the Supreme Court found applied to military commission procedures as a matter of Congress's command. The court simply did not hold that members of the Taliban rank automatically with U.S. soldiers, or that they benefit from "combatant immunity."

Further, there is good cause—in strictly counter-terrorism terms—to apply Common Article 3 to alleged members of the Taliban and al-Qaida. It is generally believed around the world that many of those detained at Guantánamo are in fact innocent of all connection with either the Taliban or al-Qaida. It is hard to imagine how a trial that does not respect "the judicial guarantees which are recognized as indispensable by civilized peoples" could convince others that Guantánamo detainees are properly detained. Unfair trials will make it more difficult to win the ideological battle at the heart of counter-terrorism.

Not Sorting Combatants from Noncombatants

Common Article 3 is especially important now because there is real doubt about whether substantial numbers of Guantánamo detainees have any connection to al-Qaida or the Taliban. Geneva tells states to take the common-sense measures of holding swift hearings on the battlefield to distinguish combatants from those swept in accidentally. But the administration decided to forego these essential procedures "to make a point—that the president can designate them all enemy combatants if he wants to." Congress and the American public are still slowly learning that Guantánamo detainees are in fact innocent of all conduct, that we have been frittering away our money, manpower and reputation not on the "worst of the worst," but on shepherds and farmers because the administration declined to sort the innocent from the guilty.

In any case, we know that "military necessity" has nothing to do with resistance to Common Article 3. As Jane Mayer recently explained in the *New Yorker*, military lawyers were wholly excluded from the rule-making process for military commissions. One military lawyer called the commissions "a political stunt. The administration clearly didn't know anything about military law or the laws of war." Those who knew most about "military necessity," in short, played no role in the decision to deviate from Common Article 3.

Adherence to Common Article 3, in line with the Supreme Court's decision in *Hamdan*, is thus not the blow to counterterrorism measures that the *Journal* claims. It is a necessary, eminently practical tool in a difficult, long-term battle. It is the line we cannot cross without losing our claim to moral and political leadership. And it is a standard we fall short of at our own risk.

> "[The Supreme Court] has formally cut the publicly accountable tie between the most fundamental political matter, namely, national survival, and the decision-making of political representatives."

The Supreme Court Has Overstepped Its Power

Andrew C. McCarthy

As an assistant United States attorney for the Southern District of New York (1993-1996), Andrew C. McCarthy led prosecution against those responsible for the 1993 bombings of the World Trade Center and other acts of terrorism. McCarthy now teaches law and acts as a political and legal commentator for the Na-tional Review and other media outlets. In the following selec-tion, McCarthy contends that the Judicial Branch of government has no role in national security; that concern falls to the Execu-tive and Legislative Branches. However, in the Hamdan v. Rums-feld *case, the Supreme Court unwisely chose to interfere with the manner in which the government pursues its war on terrorism. McCarthy sees this as an example of a new juristocracy in America, a dangerous state in which the courts will champion terrorists' rights in order to preserve what they believe is judicial authority to limit executive privilege.*

From the Founding right up until the still-quaking bomb-shell of *Hamdan v. Rumsfeld*, issued at the end of the Su-preme Court's term in late June [2006], the primary impera-

Andrew C. McCarthy, "The New Juristocracy," *New Criterion*, September 2006, pp. 65–70. Copyright © Foundation for Cultural Reviews, Inc. Reproduced by permission.

tive of national government was to protect the security of the governed from hostile outsiders. The Framers, however, had an ingenious gloss on this venerable first principle. In the great American experiment in republican democracy, this power of self-preservation—what Justice Felix Frankfurter, in another era of grave peril, called "the most pervasive aspect of sovereignty"—would repose only in those political actors directly accountable to the people whose lives hung in the balance.

The arrangement made exquisite sense. On the one hand, if the public's representatives were insufficiently attentive to national security, those with the most at stake could vote them out of office. On the other hand, if public officials failed to give due deference to the civil rights that guarantee our freedom, Americans, lovers of liberty, could show them the door. The epicenter of this dynamic would be the President of the United States, the only public official (besides the Vice President) elected by, and accountable to, all of the people.

Judges? They would have no role in national security. They, after all, are politically unaccountable. This is neither to disparage them nor suggest they are irresponsible, much less unpatriotic. They are unaccountable to the people because they are accountable only to the law. And not some universal law. They are custodians of the people's laws, those governing the domestic body politic.

Judiciary Has No Role in National Security

Those laws quite intentionally handcuff government for the sake of promoting freedom. They thus have no place in the international arena, a state of nature in which nations, insurgent militias, and, now, transnational terrorist networks all claim the right to use force. "The circumstances that endanger the safety of nations are infinite," [Alexander] Hamilton observed in *The Federalist*. "[F]or this reason no constitutional shackles can wisely be imposed on the power to which the care of it is committed."

In stark contrast, within the domestic realm, government would have a comparative monopoly on the legitimate use of force. Security would not be as pressing a concern. Within this fortress, judicial courts could guarantee *Americans* freedom from oppressive action by *their government*. They could preserve the rule of law indispensable for the *American body politic* to flourish. It was for those reasons—in abeyance of mortal danger—that the nation could afford to insulate them from popular passions, whims, and safety concerns.

However patently central it is to a good society, the judicial function remains largely irrelevant to the international order. For all the blather about our "international community," it is an ersatz community, lying beyond our laws and democratic choices. Unlike dreamy modern internationalists, the Framers well understood that broad swaths of this "community"—enemies of the United States—would always pose threats, some existential, to the body politic.

Such threats are not *legal* problems. They do not principally involve Americans being deprived of their legal entitlements by their government—the cases and controversies judicial power was designed to resolve. They are clashes between the American national community and the outside world. They are the stuff of *political* power—diplomacy, force, and all the intermediate measures wielded by the political branches. The judicial power has no place because American courts are part and parcel of the American national community; they do not exist outside or above it.

In our system, rising to external threats from alien forces with no claim on the protections of American law would be the domain of the political branches. In times of crisis and war, it would be uniquely the province of an energetic executive. All the immense might the United States could muster for its self-preservation would be concentrated in one set of hands, able to act swiftly and decisively to quell enemies endlessly variant in size, strength, and method of attack.

The President Answers to the People

Was that, as vigorously claimed by today's critics of the purportedly "imperial presidency" of George W. Bush, a blank check? Of course it was not. Those hands, the president's, answer to the American people. The line between liberty and security is not a fixed one. "The great ordinances of the Constitution," the legendary Oliver Wendell Holmes, Jr., admonished, "do not establish and divide fields of black and white." They are not amenable to static judicial formulas. Our barometer—within very wide margins—is what the American people demand for their well-being, which ebbs and flows with the state of the threat environment.

This is why, for example, we have never—at least until *Hamdan*—had a one-sided treaty with an international terrorist organization, whereby jihadists get to keep killing Americans and we guarantee them American rights. The Constitution makes treaties the province of accountable political actors. No public official who had any thought of remaining a public official would propose a departure from that principle. In the days before *Hamdan*, when the Framers' requirement of an accountability nexus between the protectors and the protected held sway, such a bizarre idea would have been a career-ender.

Judicial Intrusion Is Now the Rule

National self-preservation: the irreducible core of popular self-determination. It is simply not the business of judges. And once, in a less hubristic time, no one knew that better than the judges themselves. Of presidential power, Holmes wrote for a unanimous Supreme Court in 1909: "When it comes to a decision by the head of the State upon a matter involving its life, the ordinary rights of individuals must yield to what *he deems* the necessities of the moment. Public danger warrants *the substitution of executive process for judicial process*" (emphasis added). Justice Robert Jackson—a giant in both the accountable and unaccountable worlds, having served as FDR's

[Franklin Delano Roosevelt's] attorney general before being named to the Supreme Court and, ultimately, prosecuting the Nazis at Nuremburg—put it emphatically in 1936:

> [T]he very nature of executive decisions as to foreign policy is political, not judicial. Such decisions are wholly confided by our Constitution to the political departments of the government, Executive and Legislative. They are delicate, complex, and involve large elements of prophecy. *They are and should be undertaken only by those directly responsible to the people whose welfare they advance or imperil.* They are decisions of a kind for which *the Judiciary has neither aptitude, facilities nor responsibility* and which has long been held to belong in the *domain of political power not subject to judicial intrusion or inquiry* [italics mine].

No longer. With *Hamdan*, a very different breed of Supreme Court has ushered in a new juristocracy. It has formally cut the publicly accountable tie between the most fundamental political matter, namely, national survival, and the decision-making of political representatives. And already this much is clear: While judicial intrusion is now the order of the day, judicial aptitude has not advanced beyond Justice Jackson's low expectations.

The Juristocracy in Action

In trumping democratic self-determination, the *Hamdan* court's first order of business was to cashier Congress as an instrument of the public will. In a juristocracy, a legislature is simply a tool for imposing the judicial will on the executive— and the people. As a stricture on the judiciary itself, Congress is impotent.

In 2004, the budding juristocracy had first flexed its new wartime muscles with an unprecedented grant of American court access to alien enemy combatants (i.e., non-American terrorists) engaged in a barbaric war against Americans. Specifically, the Supreme Court held, in *Rasul v. Bush*, that

America's enemies could use America's courts to file habeas corpus petitions challenging their detention by America's military, which had been sent into battle by America's president after a sweeping authorization overwhelmingly approved by America's legislature.

Americans, it should astonish no one to learn, were not in favor. They pressed their accountable representatives to act. Congress responded with last December's [2005] Detainee Treatment Act (DTA). It provided, in no uncertain terms, that "no court, justice or judge shall have jurisdiction to hear or consider an application for a writ of habeas corpus filed by or on behalf of an alien detained by the Department of Defense at Guantanamo Bay, Cuba."

Congress, having considered the executive branch's arrangements for the detention and trial by military commission of alien combatants, determined that those military proceedings should go forward. This was unsurprising. The detention of enemy combatants is a staple of warfare. When combatants violate the laws of war—as is al Qaeda's modus operandi—military commissions have been employed since the nation's founding to try them. The commissions authorized by President Bush for al Qaeda terrorists after the 9/11 attacks were, by historic standards, remarkably deferential to fair-trial concerns—particularly given that the enemy's idea of due process for captives is to start a new videocassette before recording the next decapitation. . . .

Nevertheless, in recognition of the fact that the enemy targets civilians for mass homicide, the president factored into the fair-trial calculus the imperative of protecting the lives for which he is accountable. Thus, while combatants would presumptively have a right to be present at all stages of their trials, that presence could be denied during portions in which classified information was to be introduced (including secret methods and sources for obtaining that information).

Mind you, the combatant would not be completely shut out; his military counsel would have the right to be present. But the balance struck was to provide considerable due process while screening the enemy from intelligence vital to the national defense. Information that could be used against us in the ongoing war. Information the revelation of which might induce foreign intelligence services to refrain from cooperating with us. Information of the kind jihadists were lavishly given during the 1990s, when terrorism was regarded as a crime and al Qaeda reaped the benefits of disclosure-rich standards that govern American civilian trials.

Congress Directs the Courts to Desist

Surveying these procedures at the end of 2005, Congress clearly approved. It was, after all, within the legislature's power to condemn the commissions, or at least clarify that they were not what Congress contemplated when it broadly authorized the use of military force after the 9/11 attacks. To the contrary, the DTA patently assumed that the commissions would go forward to completion without further interference from the civilian court system. But bowing to criticism from civil liberties activists and foreign commentators, Congress balanced American national security against complaints that military proceedings were too unilaterally controlled by the executive branch. Generous provision was made for independent judicial review. . . .

It was only with those protections in place that Congress unambiguously directed the courts, including the Supreme Court, to cease and desist interfering in the executive's conduct of foreign policy and warfare. Such intrusions, as Justice Jackson had soundly referred to them, were in arrant contravention of the goal of the war, which is to defeat the enemy, not to empower him. The Supreme Court itself had acknowledged in the wake of World War II (in the 1946 *Yamashita* case) that the "trial and punishment of enemy combatants" who commit war crimes are part of the "conduct of war." The conduct of war, military necessity, is a presidential responsibility, far beyond the judicial ken.

Seeking to Undercut Presidential Power

A jurisdiction, though, abides no curbs on its jurisdiction. It matters not that the Framers made Congress the master of the courts' jurisdiction. In this juristocracy, our Constitution and congressional statutes like the DTA mean not what they say, but whatever five Supreme Court justices say that they mean. In this instance, five *Hamdan* justices led by John Paul Stevens (author of the aforementioned *Rasul* debacle), decided that "no court, justice or judge shall have jurisdiction" actually meant "we five justices shall have such jurisdiction as we damn well please." With reasoning that would make a snake-oil salesman blush, the majority ruled that the DTA was somehow meant to apply only to future detainee cases, not to detainees whose cases were pending at the time of enactment. Of course, the whole point of the DTA had been to deal with pending detainee cases—the Gitmo [Guantanamo] population is steadily dwindling and no one anticipates new cases. But such congressional shackles are gossamer against the judicial will-to-power.

Having brushed aside governing law, the juristocracy then moved on to its actual agenda: slamming the president for . . . brushing aside governing law. At least that was what the majority purported to be doing. The charge, however, is baseless. In reality, what this court has done is impose on a nation at war laws Congress never enacted, which incorporate a post-sovereign vision of human rights Americans have never adopted, derived from a treaty the United States has never ratified—indeed, has expressly rejected owing to fear that it would vest terrorists with broad legal protections.

Rewriting the Geneva Conventions

The *Hamdan* majority cashiered the Bush military commissions on the ground that they violate Common Article 3 (CA3) of the 1949 Geneva Conventions. On its face, this is preposterous, amounting to a drastic rewrite of the Conventions as ratified by the political branches through the Constitution's treaty process. Naturally, al Qaeda, being a terrorist network rather than a country, is not a Geneva signatory. CA3 operates to extend some prisoner-of-war protections to the militias of non-signatories, but only in very particular circumstances: to wit, conflicts "not of an international character occurring in the territory of one of the High Contracting Parties," meaning civil wars. To contort al Qaeda into this category, the court had to find that a terror network which has killed Americans in New York, Virginia, Somalia, Saudi Arabia, Kenya, Tanzania, Yemen, Afghanistan, and Iraq—to say nothing of the hundreds of non-Americans it has slaughtered globally—is somehow not "of an international character" because it is not a nation. Swept aside were the inconveniences that the war on terror is patently not confined to Afghanistan (where Hamdan, Osama bin Laden's personal driver, was captured), and that American courts have traditionally recognized the president's supremacy in the interpretation of treaties (which he ratifies and can unilaterally end).

More alarming, though, are the ramifications of applying CA3. Treaties are international compacts. Presumptively, they do not create private rights that can be vindicated in litigation. Disputes about their application are fodder for diplomacy—negotiations and reclamations between the political representatives of concerned states, not lawsuits. Indeed, presumptions aside, the Geneva Conventions expressly provide for non-judicial dispute resolution. This "non-self-execution" doctrine was pivotal to the unanimous rejection of Hamdan's claims by the D.C. Circuit panel (one of whose members was now-U.S. Chief Justice John Roberts—who thus recused himself from the Supreme Court's consideration of the case). Yet the Supreme Court ignored it.

U.S. Law Not Subordinate to International Law

The Court's rationale was vague. At times, the 5-3 majority seems to have held that CA3 applied not because Geneva was independently enforceable but because it was implicitly incorporated when Congress enacted the Uniform Code of Military Justice (UCMJ). This was dubious to say the least: the UCMJ, which expressly recognized the president's constitutional authority to convene military commissions, mentions not CA3 but the "law of war." It was the *Hamdan* Court that claimed this term included Geneva's CA3—a transparent cherry pick since, if the Court is right, there would be no reason "law of war" would not also include the Geneva provisions that make the treaty judicially unenforceable.

The Court was not clear that this supposed UCMJ incorporation was the only basis for making CA3 judicially enforceable. The majority elusively intimated that it could be vindicated *as a treaty* by private litigants (i.e., as if Geneva were a statute, like the Americans with Disabilities Act). This sets the stage of the next great battle for the shock troops the Hudson Institute's John Fonte has so aptly labeled "transnational progressives"—the vanguard of NGOs [nongovernmental organizations], global bureaucrats, and law professors molding a post-sovereign world based in "international human rights law." Since the 1970s, a pervasive infrastructure of such "law" has been erected. It is heavily leftist, having been drafted, for the most part, by activist NGOs. American presidents, especially Jimmy Carter, felt comfortable signing on to much of it. . . .

Case in point: the rights of alien terrorists. Beginning in the late 1970s, fully recognizing that the Geneva Conventions do not, in fact, provide protections for terrorist organizations, human rights activists sought adoption of the so-called 1977 Protocol I Additional. This Geneva supplement, however, was rejected by the [Ronald] Reagan administration. The United States determined its adoption would legitimize terrorist tactics. That is, it would have been the antithesis of the humane and civilizing inspiration for Geneva because its effect would be the encouragement of more terrorism.

Judges, Freedoms, and National Security

Thus with *Hamdan*, the unaccountable branch, the one the Framers excluded from life-and-death matters of the state, has entered the nation into the very suicidal treaty the people's elected officials sagely shunned. And what rights must be accorded under CA3 to savages seeking to supplant American democracy with a fundamentalist caliphate? Why, freedom from "outrages upon personal dignity, in particular humiliating and degrading treatment," and "all the judicial guarantees which are recognized as indispensable by civilized peoples." This is to say, capaciously promiscuous guarantees the parameters of which will eventually be determined not by those whose lives hang in the balance, but by federal judges.

There was a time, not long ago, when American courts were *our* bulwark, guaranteeing Americans a fair shake from their own government. Now, they are fast transforming into a supra-sovereign tribunal: a forum where the rest of the world, including our mortal enemies, is invited to press its case against the United States—a testament to the farcical conceit that a law degree and a prestigious judicial appointment render one fit to determine the security needs of the citizens from which one is blissfully insulated. Welcome to *Hamdan*'s new juristocracy.

"Now is the moment for comprehensive legislation to institutionalize [counterterrorism] policy for the long term."

Congress Needs a Clear Counterterrorism Policy

Kenneth Anderson

In the following viewpoint, Kenneth Anderson argues that the U.S. Supreme Court's Hamdan v. Rumsfeld *ruling illustrates that the judicial branch of government is willing to interpret constitutional law but otherwise refrain from dictating national security. This decision is appropriate, according to Anderson, because the burden of America's pursuit of the war on terror should rightfully fall on the legislative branch. In Anderson's view, Congress—which has been reluctant to define the laws needed to successfully pursue the war—must take responsibility to clarify the country's counterterrorism policies so that issues concerning the trying of prisoners and other war matters need no longer be hashed out in the courts. Kenneth Anderson is a professor of law at American University and a research fellow at the Hoover Institution as well as the operator of the* Law of War and Just War Theory Weblog.

Two branches of government have been hard at work in the war on terror these past years, even if they have not infrequently worked at cross-purposes. Executive agencies devise a warrantless surveillance program—and a federal judge declares it unconstitutional. Administration officials and federal bureaucrats devise rules for trying accused terrorists in

Kenneth Anderson, "Law and Terror," *Policy Review*, vol. 139, October 2006, pp. 3–20. Copyright © 2006 Hoover Institution. Reproduced by permission.

military tribunals—and the *Hamdan* decision sends the tribunal drafters back to the drawing board.

But where are the people's elected representatives in all of this? The Supreme Court has said that Congress has an indispensable role to play in establishing democratically legitimate policy in counterterrorism. Democratic theory tells us, moreover, that whatever actions the executive was able to undertake on its own authority in the immediate emergency of 9/11, and indeed whatever inherent powers it might permanently possess, in fact democracy is better off when the political branches work in concert to create a long term policy. So where is the legislation, passed by Congress and signed into law by the president, on the multiple topics that make up a full and complete counterterrorism policy for the country?

Hesitant to Tackle Counterterror Policy

It is true that, at this writing, Congress is finally coming to grapple with legislation proposed to regulate trials of enemy combatants and interrogation procedures. It is legislation of grave national importance. It is likewise true that Congress involved itself in counterterrorism policy in the Detainee Treatment Act of 2005 (the McCain amendment). But notwithstanding the importance of those issues, they are in fact narrow ones. They are merely compelled by the *Hamdan* decision, and far from the range or depth of issues necessary to establish what the country urgently needs prior to the end of the [George W.] Bush second term, and what the Bush administration ought to have been working toward from the day its second term began—a long term, systematic, comprehensive, institutionalized counterterrorism policy for the United States.

Unfortunately, despite the end-of-term, politically charged pre-election legislative bustle, there is no indication that Congress has any appetite to undertake systematic, comprehensive legislation with respect to counterterrorism policy. Nor is there any indication that the George W. Bush administration has any desire to seek it. No one should mistake the energetic debate of this moment—debate in which, in any case, Democrats are not really taking part—for more than what it is. The legislative proposals of both the administration and its interlocutors hew narrowly to the *Hamdan* minimum—another skirmish, in other words, not over concrete policy in the war on terror, but instead in the never-ending, abstract, and finally metaphysical battle over the constitutional extent of presidential discretion. But what the administration especially fails to appreciate is that no matter who wins the 2008 presidential election or the 2006 midterms, there is not likely to *be* any coherent national counterterrorism policy past the end of the second Bush administration unless Congress takes steps to legislate it, institutionalize it, and make it long-term and indeed permanent.

The Judiciary's Role

The fissured *Hamdan* decision, while leaving open many momentous questions, at least makes one thing reasonably clear: Responsibility for democratically establishing the war on terror—its overall contours, its long-term legitimacy, its institutional form, its trade-offs of values of national security and civil liberties—today falls to the legislative branch. The most desirable policy result of *Hamdan* would be the acknowledgment that the judiciary has only a limited role to play in foreign policy and national security, and that it will discipline itself to stay out of such disputes. At the same time, the judiciary will stay out of these arenas because it knows that the separation of powers will remain in the two political branches of government operating actively as checks and balances upon each other.

That interpretation of *Hamdan* is in accordance with the best interpretation of a long line of Supreme Court cases dealing with the role of the judiciary in time of war and in matters of urgent national security: Rather than dealing with the substantive result, the Court appears often to have been concerned instead with ensuring that meaningful democratic checks and balances are maintained even if the courts stay out, through the active participation of Congress in legislation. And in any case, that is the democratically legitimate thing to do for long-term policy, even vital matters of national security, in the American republic.

Executive vs. Judicial

The strategic political situation is simple and unattractive. The administration remains caught in the grip of a lawyerly clique that places an abstract ideology of executive discretion above the war on terror and is willing to lose intragovernmental battles about how to conduct the latter over and over again for the sake of the former. The administration therefore brings only minimal legislation to Congress, preferring to bet on arguments of executive power that are rebuffed in the courts. The Supreme Court gives some indication that it is willing to lessen its role in what amounts to foreign policy and war, provided the two political branches come together to give the democratic imprimatur of legislation to counterterrorism policy and to the inevitable trade-offs between national security and civil liberties. Congress, however, has little desire to exert itself legislatively in these matters because, despite the noise it makes in the public sphere, it currently has the best of all worlds—the ability to snipe, second-guess, complain, whine, and Monday-morning-quarterback against the administration, without any obligation to legislate what it thinks the solution should actually be. The executive allows it to do so, up to now, because it believes—quite fantastically—that it is protecting and even enhancing executive power for the long run. And this is a House and Senate whose majorities, for the moment, are of the president's own party. Whining without accountability—Congress wallows, one might be forgiven for thinking, precisely in its element. And why would it want to do anything different? It is a good bet that *Hamdan* 's requirements can be satisfied with relatively modest legislative changes—and a bad bet that Congress will be eager to undertake more, before or after the midterm elections.

Strategically, this frozen state of affairs unfortunately makes good sense, from Congress's self-absorbed and self-interested point of view. It is, however, a terrible mistake from the standpoint of policy and the common good of the American people. This is not merely because so many of President Bush's opponents believe the very idea of a "war" on terror to be an appalling, if not absurd, policy. Opponents of the Bush administration seek a counterterrorism policy that emphasizes containment of the terrorist threat—in the short to medium term, a defensive posture emphasizing such elements as control over vital entry points such as seaports, counterterrorism pursued as criminal justice domestically, police and intelligence cooperation with allied governments abroad and, in the longer term, reaching out culturally and socially to the Muslim world, seeking a permanent solution to the Israeli-Palestinian conflict, and hoping that a posture of restraint, rather than bellicose reaction, will result in a diminution of global anti-Americanism among inflamed Muslim populations that feed the ranks of Islamofascist terrorists. It seeks to decouple the Bush administration's linkage of terrorists and rogue states with weapons of mass destruction, and it argues that war cannot contain terrorism, nor can war democratize the Middle East, in Iraq or anywhere else. The terminology of a "war on terrorism" is, on this view, tendentious, because it illegitimately gives standing to war as counterterrorism policy, whereas that is precisely what should be at issue. The phrase "war on terror" presumes the conclusion of what should be a policy debate.

Bush's Aggressive Counterterrorism Policy

The Bush administration and its supporters do not deny the value of any of these elements of a counterterrorism strategy.

Cooperation with allies in intelligence and police work is undeniably important, likewise control over ports and other points of entry and—many would add, although the Bush administration's bona fides on this point are themselves at issue—the U.S. land borders generally. Who would not like to see a diminution of anti-Americanism in the Muslim world, whether in the Middle East, Muslim Europe, or elsewhere? Who would not like to see a permanent solution to the Israeli-Palestinian conflict? The extra elements under debate, the additions of the Bush administration to this list, are two—war, the willingness to use military force, for a variety of purposes and, second, the aggressive use of intelligence-gathering methods, including aggressive interrogation falling short of torture. The president has made the case in his speeches for the indispensability of these aggressive methods in preventing terrorist attacks. One may regard the trade-off he implicitly proposes between the human rights of terrorist suspects and security as morally wrong. But his description of the concrete stakes is surely right, and those who might regard his language as merely hyperbolic take American and other lives in their hands. And looking to the new U.S. counterterrorism strategy unrolled at the beginning of September [2006] by the administration along with other parts of its campaign to refocus on the war on terror, the Bush administration sees war as a means to deny terrorists safe haven, to establish to the world that harboring terrorists risks war, to ensure that terrorists do not have access to weapons of mass destruction, and to topple evil regimes with the aim of introducing democracy in the hopes of breaking the cycle of corrupt, authoritarian regimes that motivate terrorism. More generally, the inclusion of war as an instrument of counterterrorism policy is a way of remaining on offense, rather than defense, carrying the battle to the terrorists themselves, rather than waiting for them to come to us. . . .

Of course, sensible people on either side of this debate recognize that the world cannot be understood in simple binaries of war and not-war. Sensible people do not think solely about counterterrorism as offense or defense, criminal justice or war containment or regime change. It is a question of emphasis and the mix of tools available. Nonetheless, the two are fundamentally distinguished by two characteristics: whether war and the large-scale use of military force shall be a tool of counterterrorism policy or not, and whether intelligence gathering shall include aggressive techniques even though still falling short of torture. It might develop in the future that the disputants disagree on some other fundamental issue, such as the role and permissibility of armed violence falling short of war—targeted assassinations or abductions by intelligence agents, for example. But nearly all the other instruments of policy are agreed upon by the serious parties as useful and important. The points of disagreement are war and the permissible extent of intelligence gathering. Those issues define the two sides, no matter what the other complexities. The result is that each alternative form of counterterrorism sets forth a complex bet, filled with guesses and unknowns about what is most likely to protect American security over the long term. As such, neither one can be written off as obviously foolish. And yet decisions have to be made between them. . . .

The State of Emergency Will Not Last

All of which makes it more dismaying that Congress should respond so minimally to the democratic challenge of defining counterterrorism policy, comprehensively and for the long term, all the more dismaying that the Bush administration should have avoided taking up comprehensive policy with the national legislature. Like most readers of this essay, I have a view on the fundamental approach to counterterrorism policy; I reckon it a war and reckon the Bush administration's approach better than the Democratic Party alternative. Speaking, however, not as a supporter of the Bush administration's war on terror but instead as a democrat, someone committed to democratic process, it seems to me less important at this moment in the political cycle to argue for a particular policy in counterterrorism policy—a war on terror or something else—than to argue that now is the moment for comprehensive legislation to institutionalize policy for the long term.

Irrespective of where one comes down in the debate over counterterrorism policy, Congress today should act maximally through the only legitimate mechanism for the long haul in a democracy, legislation. No matter who is in control of the House or Senate come January 2007, it is critical that the legislature step up to its democratic responsibility. The administration responded swiftly to an unprecedented national emergency. But the United States cannot operate permanently as a national security state. The Cold War demonstrated that a democracy *can* develop mechanisms to accommodate—so long as the democratic apparatus remains flexible and willing to recognize the need for genuine tradeoffs—national security, democratic process, and civil liberties. The Bush administration has operated national security questions and the war on terror, in [journalist] Jonathan Rauch's words, "out of its hip pocket," on a discretionary basis. But that cannot be the long-term operation of a democracy. I am willing to do political battle in favor of a genuine "war" on terror; but more important at this moment is the democratic impulse—that the republic, and its legislature, move beyond the executive discretion suitable to an emergency and act in the way a democracy constitutionally possessed of a legislature should act. . . .

A Law Specific to the Extraordinary Threat

As a general principle on which comprehensive legislation should be based, counterterrorism laws which then morph into general criminal law are a very bad idea. Either they will indeed erode ordinary civil liberties, or else they are laws

[that] make sense in limited application to the extraordinary threat of terrorism but nonetheless will not get passed because of the fear of more general application. The point is to draft legislation to cover contingencies that are indeed considered extraordinary with respect to ordinary criminals and ordinary crimes. For that reason, in some cases—as in tribunals for alleged terrorists—they justify procedures involving special rules that deliberately depart from the usual rules of criminal law. Perhaps any such departures are all a mistake and, as many have argued, all of this should be undertaken in the regular law courts under regular laws of the land or not at all. And perhaps Congress would agree—although I doubt it. I take as point of departure for the remainder of this discussion that certain aspects of counterterrorism policy may, as a practical necessity, differ from the usual systems of criminal justice and enforcement. If, even only for argument's sake, that is accepted, however, then at least the circumstances under which those exceptional rules may be invoked should be confined strictly to the emergency which justified them in the first place—viz., terrorism strictly, and nothing else. Not even child pornography or whatever admittedly heinous crime might otherwise tempt departure from normal processes. Rules for a state of exception must remain rules solely for the stated exception.

The justification for a strict separation of ordinary law and counterterrorism regimes has a conceptual basis. Transnational terrorists are, on the one hand, criminals who use or hope to use the basest criminal means—the slaughter of innocents to leverage political gains. So they *are* criminals. But that does not automatically mean that they thereby merit access to the ordinary criminal law system that we, as a domestic society, have elaborated to deal with those of our own who criminally deviate from the legal and social order. Our system of criminal justice is aimed fundamentally at those within our own political community, within our own domestic society, who transgress its norms. Ordinary criminals violate our society's legal norms; they do not challenge, much less attack with terrorist violence, its fundamental legitimacy and existence. The terrorists who attack us, on the contrary, are not merely criminals—they are simultaneously our "enemies." They are enemies of the social and legal order itself, not merely deviants within it.

Eroding Civil Liberties

The consequences of seeking to deal with terrorists who are at once "criminals and enemies" through a system of criminal justice designed with ordinary criminals in mind are severe. We risk dragging down the entire criminal justice system to the level necessary—and justified—to contain the terrorist threat, or else we risk not dealing with the terrorist threat at all. The manifest difficulties of the [Zacarias] Moussaoui trial [i.e., the trial of the first al Qaeda conspirator to be arraigned in the United Sates] demonstrate just how unsuited the ordinary mechanisms of criminal justice are for dealing with alleged terrorists; likewise the hubris of prosecutors in always thinking they will be the ones who manage to make the case and claim the glory in the newspapers. . . .

Important civil liberties we cherish—and some civil liberties embedded in criminal law dating from the [chief justice Earl] Warren Court [1953–1969] that some conservatives dispute but I, at least, cherish—*will not* survive contact with a flood of serious terrorism cases. And just as the Patriot Act's presumably "anti-terror" provisions leak over to other crimes, such as child porn, trying our terrorism cases in ordinary courts will tend to diminish our civil liberties in ordinary cases as well. When it comes to those who are *not* criminals and enemies to our political community, when it comes to those who "merely" deviate from our social order, even in very serious and violent ways, we owe it to them and to ourselves—we owe it to "us" as a people—not to sacrifice the nobler aims of criminal justice, including rehabilitation, because we have no choice but harshness in dealing with terrorists. It is not, as some might imagine, merely a matter of necessity in dealing with terrorism—it is, rather, a general moral proposition that we do not owe those who declare themselves enemies of our constitutional political community, and then pursue their "war" with the most criminal means, the same moral or political obligations we owe to "our" ordinary criminals.

Setting Up Special Counterterrorist Courts

Because of this distinction, Congress ought to create a special terrorism court system, outside the ordinary criminal justice system, with special rules of procedure and evidence, for dealing with those accused of a strictly defined list of terrorist crimes; models can partly be found in Western Europe. The court would be civilian in nature, rather than the military tribunals currently contemplated; it would deal with persons accused of terrorism crimes who were either noncitizens or U.S. citizens, whether captured abroad or within the territorial U.S. Military tribunals would be limited to those, whether U.S. citizens or not, captured on the battlefield as traditionally defined—Iraq or Afghanistan, for example—rather than the "world as battlefield" concept of the war on terror. The court would have two hearing functions. The first would be to determine innocence, guilt, and punishment for unprivileged belligerency and any related crimes, such as murder, etc. The second would be to determine whether a detainee posed a threat to the United States—in proceedings on a regular, ongoing basis—and providing for administrative detention in such cases until the threat abated. (Citizenship would continue to differentiate rights in certain cases; and habeas corpus would be available with limitations.) As to the thorny procedural questions for a court departing ordinary U.S. criminal practice, guidance could be sought in Western European systems of terrorism courts and administrative detention, as well as the U.S. military tribunals now being legislated. As for evidentiary questions, a useful source would be the evidentiary codes of the Yugoslavia tribunal—loudly endorsed at its inception by human rights monitors—allowing for the use of hearsay evidence, anonymous witnesses, closed hearings, and generally anything that the judges thought would be of probative value; those terms would perhaps suffice and have already gained the human rights community's approval over many years.

Cautioning Against Wasteful Bureaucracies

A second way in which comprehensive counterterrorism legislation might be conceived is as a matter of large scale institutional design. What new or reformed institutions are needed to combat terror in the long run? The United States has gone down that road several times since September 11, notably in the creation of the Department of Homeland Security (DHS). It has also had numerous commissions, studies, investigations, and large-scale reports recommending many reforms to existing institutions that deal with counterterrorism. Of course it is true that Congress must have important things to say and enact with respect to any shifts in large counterterrorism bureaucracies, whether in law enforcement, intelligence, the military or elsewhere, if for no other reason than as a prerogative of its spending power. On the other hand, the experience of intelligence and counterterrorism reform, . . . provide grounds for great caution in encouraging Congress to become directly the architect of institutional design for counterterrorism. . . .

Fighting the Ideological War

Congress instead has a far more important role that only it can play. Among all the possible topics of legislation, all the things that Congress might do, those that matter most are not matters of either institutional design or management but values. Our values; America's values—the clear enunciation of those values, what they are and our willingness to defend them.

The Islamofascist threat is potent for the long term in part because it is, as with all persistent terrorist movements, an ideology founded on values. Islamist jihadism is founded on values, ideas, beliefs, spirituality, sacrifice, martyrdom, transcendence, and eschatology that accepts a very long-term perspective; these make it dangerous because it is not amenable to the usual rationality of a democratic society, the civil society of a "polite and polished commercial people," as [philosopher of the Scottish Enlightenment] Adam Ferguson long ago described the rising bourgeois ideal in Western societies. Although it might simply burn itself out within the internal dynamics of the global Muslim communities—the past five years as a kind of extended 1968, the radical moment of an enormous Muslim baby boom cohort worldwide in a world where other societies are instead aging, but one that thankfully fades—well, that is a slender hope and not one upon which to rest political safety.

But precisely because it is driven by values, the opposition to it must likewise be driven by values. This is a vital lesson of the Cold War; [the editor of the *New Republic*,] Peter Beinart is profoundly correct to assert Islamofascism as the rise of a new totalitarianism in our time, and just as the role of Western liberal, democratic values publicly asserted is widely acknowledged in the defeat of Soviet communism, likewise the role of Western liberal, democratic values publicly asserted will be one day undisputable in the defeat of radical Islamist jihad.

In fact, the most bitter and divisive debates over national security policy and counterterrorism have been about our values—what they are and what they concretely mean in counterterrorism. Not at the level of lofty, but necessarily abstract, speeches about defending American values to which everyone can easily sign on—but instead the concrete practices of the United States government in dealing with terrorists and suspected terrorists. Issues of detention and interrogation, allegations of torture and war crimes—while keeping America safe from attack. The bitter, ugly fights over Guantanamo [prison for detainees captured in the war on terror], Abu Ghraib [prison in Iraq where Iraqi detainees were subjected to abuse by U.S. military personnel], CIA secret "black sites" in Europe, torture, rendition, putting a pure conception of the humane rule of law on one side and the specter of catastrophic terrorist attack on the other—well, liberty and security are both liberal values, both social goods, and yet in important respects fundamentally incommensurable, apples and oranges. It is no surprise that the battles over them are as deep and bitter as they are.

Yet we are not weakened by debate, even ugly debate that in the way of the lively, crude, often rude society America has always been. We are, however, weakened by the failure to resolve that debate in the only legitimate mechanism of a democracy, by democratic votes by the people's representatives. What matters is not that some people believe with all their hearts that the Bush administration has betrayed the country's values and made it complicit with torture, or that other people believe equally strongly that there are foolish and immoral Americans who would give up a million lives rather than waterboard [a form of torture] one known terrorist—what matters, rather, is that between the administration and Congress, those fundamental conflicts of values have not been brought plainly and openly before the people's representatives for votes. The republic is deeply divided; we have one and only one long-term, legitimate procedure for resolving those differences: to put the alternatives to a vote by the legislature. We have not used it—Congress has been happy, by and large, with an arrangement in which the administration does not bring these questions to them, and the administration has been happy, by and large, to keep policy in its own hands.

American Values Must Be Clarified in Laws

And so the values questions fester. And, in their own way, they undermine the ability of even the apparently purely managerial and technocratic servants of the war on terror successfully to do their work. For their work, try as one might, cannot be divorced from the values at stake. The concrete actions of CIA employees on a daily basis—who is detained, how they are treated in interrogations, whether they are released—make that only too clear. The failure to articulate clear legal standards as has been the case up to now means one of two very dangerous things—either that intelligence personnel believe that they have carte blanche in dealing with terrorist suspects or, more likely, that any action might be later regarded as criminal, resulting in an unwillingness to interrogate at all— what, after all, is the precise meaning of "degrading" treatment, violation of which might well be criminal? Can one know in advance what it would mean . . .? We all know these concerns; the president himself said so in [a] speech calling for immunity for CIA and other officials for past actions.

But the point is that this apparently technocratic gap in the ability to manage counterterrorism arises specifically from a failure to articulate our values *as law* in the war on terror. Although taking the Bush administration's point that constitutionally it lies with the executive to interpret treaty obligations, including those arising from the Geneva Conventions' Common Article Three, the very concept of the rule of law requires that acts incurring criminal or civil liability be spelled out in plain terms so as to announce in advance what is and is not legal. The very concept of the democratic rule of law requires that they be spelled out by a legislature. The vague terms of Common Article Three will of necessity be interpreted and given concrete meaning by someone—if not by

Congress, then by a judge in a case against a CIA officer. Those in Congress arguing that the executive already has sufficient authority to interpret those terms by getting—ludicrously—an opinion from a lawyer in the Justice Department, but then anticipate that liability might attach to a different interpretation given them by a judge in a criminal trial, weaken the rule of law. . . . The rule of law is undermined, and the war on terror, too, as the ability to gather intelligence is lost. Those in the administration arguing—before the White House decided that legal certainty in this case was more important than executive power—that the executive had power to determine the meanings of terms in Common Article Three forget that it is a large step from the interpretation of treaty provisions to defining the terms of actual criminal liability; the latter is surely a responsibility of the legislature. Congress ought not to be let off the hook in stating plainly—without recourse to euphemisms, platitudes, generalities, or abstractions—precisely and specifically which interrogation techniques are legal and which illegal, whether under the rubric of Common Article Three or anything else. The White House should welcome this sharing of moral responsibility for these profound and controversial choices about our collective values.

U.S. Policy Must Be Clear and Consistent

And we incur damage from our failure to convey a clear message as to our values to the outside world. It is not, to be sure, that the outside world will agree, like, or express joy at a plain, legislated U.S. policy enunciating our values and striking our bargains between the incommensurate social goods of liberty and security—the outside world will always complain, if only to seek leverage over U.S. policy—but clear evidence that this is policy of the United States and not merely a frolic of the Bush administration can only strengthen our hand against our enemies in the world. We recall that terrorist exhortations among themselves have emphasized patience to simply outwait this administration. The message that American resolve will last beyond 2008—in whatever form policy actually takes as legislation, including, come to that, policies that depart from what this administration desires—can only come from the legislature.

CHAPTER 4

Can Suspected Terrorists Be Held Indefinitely Without Charge?

Case Overview:
Boumediene et al. v. Bush (2008) and *Al Odah et al. v. United States* (2008)

Soon after the September 11, 2001, terrorist attacks upon the United States, American intelligence networks began investigating all leads that hinted at further strikes against U.S. targets. In October, intelligence officers working at the American embassy in Sarajevo, Bosnia, noted frequent telephone calls from a Muslim suspect under surveillance and parties in Pakistan and Afghanistan. Urged by American authorities, the Bosnian police arrested Bensayah Belkacem and five of his friends. All of the men were of Algerian descent, and five claimed Bosnian citizenship. They were accused of plotting to bomb the embassy. Each denied the charge and claimed to have no connection to al Qaeda, the organization that carried out the September attacks.

Despite their protests of innocence, the men were held by Bosnian authorities for three months, stripped of their citizenship and awaiting deportation. But in January 2002, the Bosnian Supreme Court was informed that there was no evidence to warrant continued detention, so the justices ordered that the men be set free and not deported. However, within hours of the ruling, Bosnian police turned the six men over to American authorities who transported them to the detention facilities at Guantánamo Naval Base in Cuba. Since then, the Algerian Six—as the press have dubbed them—have remained in lock-up despite the findings of the Bosnian Supreme Court and calls for their release by various amnesty groups and other organizations.

In summer 2004—three years after their initial detention—the Algerian Six were permitted contact with legal counsel. American lawyers filed habeas corpus claims to challenge the fact that the men had been imprisoned for years without being formally charged with a crime. Combatant Status Review Tribunals (CSRTs) run by the military affirmed that the men were properly categorized as enemy combatants based on classified evidence, but the courts waffled on whether the plaintiffs had a case. Eventually in February 2007, a U.S. court of appeals concluded that the Military Commissions Act of 2006 denied the courts jurisdiction to hear pleas from enemy combatants. The plaintiffs' attorneys petitioned for the case to be heard by the U.S. Supreme Court.

In April 2007, the Supreme Court declined to hear the case but two months later reversed its decision. Some observers suggest that it was the testimony of Stephen Abraham that swayed the justices. Abraham is a lawyer and an officer in the army reserve who was part of the CSRT system. He became disenchanted with CSRT procedures when he found that these tribunals were not privy to all the evidence that might affect the classification of Guantánamo detainees as enemy combatants. His brief description of his experiences was tendered in June to the Supreme Court in hopes of gaining its review of the appellate court's ruling. The case went forward as *Lakhdar Boumediene et al. v. George W. Bush* (Boumediene is one of the Algerian Six). In addition, the Supreme Court decided to consolidate *Boumediene* with a similar plea for habeas corpus relief in the case of *Khaled A.F. al Odah et al. v. United States.* (The plaintiffs in this case are twelve Kuwaiti nationals held at Guantánamo and their friends and relations.)

While the government claims that the hearing violates the Military Commissions Act, the plaintiffs' prosecutors in these cases have chosen to question whether it is legal for the act to deny the Court jurisdiction in such matters. Opening arguments were heard in early December 2007.

On June 12, 2008, the Court ruled in favor of the petitioners, ruling that Guantánamo detainees have constitutional rights to challenge their detention there in U.S. courts. Justice

Anthony Kennedy wrote for the Court, which was split in its ruling 5–4, emphasizing the fundamental importance of the right to habeas corpus. The ruling also addressed the separation-of-powers vital to the constitution, with Justice Kennedy noting: "To hold that the political branches may switch the Constitution on or off at will would lead to a regime in which, they, not this court, say 'what the law is.'" Joining in the majority opinion were Justices John Paul Stevens, Stephen G. Breyer, Ruth Bader Ginsburg, and David H. Souter.

Dissenting from the opinion were Chief Justice John G. Roberts and Justices Samuel A. Alito, Antonin Scalia, and Clarence Thomas. Notably, Justice Scalia commented on how the court was divided on legal as well as emotional lines, stating that the ruling "will almost certainly cause more American's to get killed" and "the nation will live to regret what the court has done today." Chief Justice Roberts maintained that the congress had enacted reasonable measures for the enemy combatants and "the majority merely replaces a review system designed by the people's representatives with a set of shapeless procedures to be defined by federal courts at some future date."

The ramifications of the Court's decision remain to be seen. Politicians and pundits alike are mixed on whether the ruling makes America more vulnerable and what, if any, impact the ruling has on military tribunals and current hearings. Underlying the ruling, most commentators view *Boumediene* and *Al-Odah* as another example of the ongoing struggle between the judicial and executive branches of government over the right to indefinitely detain prisoners of the war on terror. Some, however, fear that the jockeying for authority masks more troubling questions about the evidence used to arrest these detainees and about possible torture during their incarceration.

> *"The laws and Constitution are designed to survive, and remain in force, in extraordinary times."*

The Court's Decision: Terror Suspects Must Be Afforded Habeas Corpus

Anthony M. Kennedy

In 2007, the Supreme Court consolidated Boumediene v. Bush *and* al Odah v. United States *under* Boumediene v. Bush. *In both cases, the petitioners were terror suspects held at the Guantanamo Bay naval base in Cuba. In a split decision—5 to 4—the court ruled that the Detainee Treatment Act of 2005 and the Military Commissions Act of 2006 did not adequately provide detainees with a means to challenge their detention. Anthony Kennedy writes for the majority in the following Supreme Court decision, emphasizing the fundamental importance of habeas corpus rights, even in times where the country is at war. This decision defends the right of habeas corpus for all Guantanamo Bay prisoners. Anthony Kennedy was appointed to the Supreme Court in 1988, and has been important as the Court's swing vote in many close decisions.*

Petitioners are aliens designated as enemy combatants and detained at the United States Naval Station at Guantanamo Bay, Cuba. There are others detained there, also aliens, who are not parties to this suit.

Petitioners present a question not resolved by our earlier cases relating to the detention of aliens at Guantanamo:

Anthony M. Kennedy, majority opinion, *Boumediene v. Bush* and *al Odah v. United States*, June 12, 2008.

whether they have the constitutional privilege of habeas corpus, a privilege not to be withdrawn except in conformance with the Suspension Clause. We hold these petitioners do have the habeas corpus privilege. Congress has enacted a statute, the Detainee Treatment Act of 2005 (DTA) that provides certain procedures for review of the detainees' status. We hold that those procedures are not an adequate and effective substitute for habeas corpus. Therefore §7 of the Military Commissions Act of 2006 (MCA), operates as an unconstitutional suspension of the writ. We do not address whether the President has authority to detain these petitioners nor do we hold that the writ must issue. These and other questions regarding the legality of the detention are to be resolved in the first instance by the District Court. . . .

Attributes of Adequate Habeas Corpus Proceedings

We do not endeavor to offer a comprehensive summary of the requisites for an adequate substitute for habeas corpus. We do consider it uncontroversial, however, that the privilege of habeas corpus entitles the prisoner to a meaningful opportunity to demonstrate that he is being held pursuant to "the erroneous application or interpretation" of relevant law. And the habeas court must have the power to order the conditional release of an individual unlawfully detained—though release need not be the exclusive remedy and is not the appropriate one in every case in which the writ is granted. These are the easily identified attributes of any constitutionally adequate habeas corpus proceeding. But, depending on the circumstances, more may be required. . . .

Where a person is detained by executive order, rather than, say, after being tried and convicted in a court, the need for collateral review is most pressing. A criminal conviction in the usual course occurs after a judicial hearing before a tribunal disinterested in the outcome and committed to procedures designed to ensure its own independence. These dynamics are not inherent in executive detention orders or executive review procedures. In this context the need for habeas corpus is more urgent. The intended duration of the detention and the reasons for it bear upon the precise scope of the inquiry. Habeas corpus proceedings need not resemble a criminal trial, even when the detention is by executive order. But the writ must be effective. The habeas court must have sufficient authority to conduct a meaningful review of both the cause for detention and the Executive's power to detain.

Evaluation of the Combatant Status Review Tribunals

To determine the necessary scope of habeas corpus review, therefore, we must assess the CSRT [Combatant Status Review Tribunals] process, the mechanism through which petitioners' designation as enemy combatants became final. . . .

Petitioners identify what they see as myriad deficiencies in the CSRTs. The most relevant for our purposes are the constraints upon the detainee's ability to rebut the factual basis for the Government's assertion that he is an enemy combatant. As already noted, at the CSRT stage the detainee has limited means to find or present evidence to challenge the Government's case against him. He does not have the assistance of counsel and may not be aware of the most critical allegations that the Government relied upon to order his detention. The detainee can confront witnesses that testify during the CSRT proceedings. But given that there are in effect no limits on the admission of hearsay evidence—the only requirement is that the tribunal deem the evidence "relevant and helpful"—the detainee's opportunity to question witnesses is likely to be more theoretical than real.

The Government defends the CSRT process, arguing that it was designed to conform to the procedures suggested by the plurality in *Hamdi v. Rumsfeld* (2004). Setting aside the fact that the relevant language in *Hamdi* did not garner a majority of the Court, it does not control the matter at hand. None of the parties in *Hamdi* argued there had been a suspension of the writ. Nor could they. The §2241 habeas corpus process remained in place. Accordingly, the plurality concentrated on whether the Executive had the authority to detain and, if so, what rights the detainee had under the Due Process Clause. True, there are places in the *Hamdi* plurality opinion where it is difficult to tell where its extrapolation of §2241 ends and its analysis of the petitioner's Due Process rights begins. But the Court had no occasion to define the necessary scope of habeas review, for Suspension Clause purposes, in the context of enemy combatant detentions. The closest the plurality came to doing so was in discussing whether, in light of separation-of-powers concerns, §2241 should be construed to forbid the District Court from inquiring beyond the affidavit Hamdi's custodian provided in answer to the detainee's habeas petition. The plurality answered this question with an emphatic "no."

Even if we were to assume that the CSRTs satisfy due process standards, it would not end our inquiry. Habeas corpus is a collateral process that exists, in Justice Holmes' words, to "cu[t] through all forms and g[o] to the very tissue of the structure. It comes in from the outside, not in subordination to the proceedings, and although every form may have been preserved opens the inquiry whether they have been more than an empty shell." Even when the procedures authorizing detention are structurally sound, the Suspension Clause remains applicable and the writ relevant. This is so, as *Hayman v. United States* (1952) and *Swain v. Pressley* (1977) [the two leading cases addressing habeas substitutes] make clear, even where the prisoner is detained after a criminal trial conducted in full accordance with the protections of the Bill of Rights. Were this not the case, there would have been no reason for the Court to inquire into the adequacy of substitute habeas procedures in *Hayman* and *Swain*. That the prisoners were detained pursuant to the most rigorous proceedings imaginable, a full criminal trial, would have been enough to render any habeas substitute acceptable per se.

Although we make no judgment as to whether the CSRTs, as currently constituted, satisfy due process standards, we agree with petitioners that, even when all the parties involved in this process act with diligence and in good faith, there is considerable risk of error in the tribunal's findings of fact. This is a risk inherent in any process that, in the words of the former Chief Judge of the Court of Appeals, is "closed and accusatorial." And given that the consequence of error may be detention of persons for the duration of hostilities that may last a generation or more, this is a risk too significant to ignore.

For the writ of habeas corpus, or its substitute, to function as an effective and proper remedy in this context, the court that conducts the habeas proceeding must have the means to correct errors that occurred during the CSRT proceedings. This includes some authority to assess the sufficiency of the Government's evidence against the detainee. It also must have the authority to admit and consider relevant exculpatory evidence that was not introduced during the earlier proceeding. Federal habeas petitioners long have had the means to supplement the record on review, even in the postconviction habeas setting. Here that opportunity is constitutionally required. . . .

Does the Court of Appeals Meet Standards Outlined Here?

The DTA does not explicitly empower the Court of Appeals to order the applicant in a DTA review proceeding released should the court find that the standards and procedures used at his CSRT hearing were insufficient to justify detention. This is troubling. Yet, for present purposes, we can assume congressional silence permits a constitutionally required remedy. In that case it would be possible to hold that a remedy of release is impliedly provided for. The DTA might be read, furthermore, to allow the petitioners to assert most, if not all, of the legal claims they seek to advance, including their most basic claim: that the President has no authority under the AUMF [Authorization for the Use of Military Force] to detain them indefinitely. At oral argument, the Solicitor General urged us to adopt both these constructions, if doing so would allow MCA §7 to remain intact.

The absence of a release remedy and specific language allowing AUMF challenges are not the only constitutional infirmities from which the statute potentially suffers, however. The more difficult question is whether the DTA permits the Court of Appeals to make requisite findings of fact. The DTA enables petitioners to request "review" of their CSRT determination in the Court of Appeals; but the "Scope of Review" provision confines the Court of Appeals' role to reviewing whether the CSRT followed the "standards and procedures" issued by the Department of Defense and assessing whether those "standards and procedures" are lawful. Among these standards is "the requirement that the conclusion of the Tribunal be supported by a preponderance of the evidence... allowing a rebuttable presumption in favor of the Government's evidence."

Assuming the DTA can be construed to allow the Court of Appeals to review or correct the CSRT's factual determinations, as opposed to merely certifying that the tribunal applied the correct standard of proof, we see no way to construe the statute to allow what is also constitutionally required in this context: an opportunity for the detainee to present relevant exculpatory evidence that was not made part of the record in the earlier proceedings.

On its face the statute allows the Court of Appeals to consider no evidence outside the CSRT record. In the parallel litigation, however, the Court of Appeals determined that the DTA allows it to order the production of all "'reasonably available information in the possession of the U. S. Government bearing on the issue of whether the detainee meets the criteria to be designated as an enemy combatant,'" regardless of whether this evidence was put before the CSRT. The Government, with support from five members of the Court of Appeals, disagrees with this interpretation. For present purposes, however, we can assume that the Court of Appeals was correct that the DTA allows introduction and consideration of relevant exculpatory evidence that was "reasonably available" to the Government at the time of the CSRT but not made part of the record. Even so, the DTA review proceeding falls short of being a constitutionally adequate substitute, for the detainee still would have no opportunity to present evidence discovered after the CSRT proceedings concluded.

Deficiencies in the CSRT Proceeding May Be Remedied

Under the DTA the Court of Appeals has the power to review CSRT determinations by assessing the legality of standards and procedures. This implies the power to inquire into what happened at the CSRT hearing and, perhaps, to remedy certain deficiencies in that proceeding. But should the Court of Appeals determine that the CSRT followed appropriate and lawful standards and procedures, it will have reached the limits of its jurisdiction. There is no language in the DTA that can be construed to allow the Court of Appeals to admit and consider newly discovered evidence that could not have been made part of the CSRT record because it was unavailable to either the Government or the detainee when the CSRT made its findings. This evidence, however, may be critical to the detainee's argument that he is not an enemy combatant and there is no cause to detain him.

This is not a remote hypothetical. One of the petitioners, Mohamed Nechla, requested at his CSRT hearing that the Government contact his employer. The petitioner claimed the employer would corroborate Nechla's contention he had no affiliation with al Qaeda. Although the CSRT determined this testimony would be relevant, it also found the witness was not reasonably available to testify at the time of the hearing. Petitioner's counsel, however, now represents the witness is available to be heard. If a detainee can present reasonably available evidence demonstrating there is no basis for his continued detention, he must have the opportunity to present this evidence to a habeas corpus court. Even under the Court of Appeals' generous construction of the DTA, however, the evidence identified by Nechla would be inadmissible in a DTA review proceeding. . . .

By foreclosing consideration of evidence not presented or reasonably available to the detainee at the CSRT proceedings, the DTA disadvantages the detainee by limiting the scope of collateral review to a record that may not be accurate or complete. In other contexts, e.g., in post-trial habeas cases where the prisoner already has had a full and fair opportunity to develop the factual predicate of his claims, similar limitations on the scope of habeas review may be appropriate. In this context, however, where the underlying detention proceedings lack the necessary adversarial character, the detainee cannot be held responsible for all deficiencies in the record.

The Government does not make the alternative argument that the DTA allows for the introduction of previously unavailable exculpatory evidence on appeal. It does point out, however, that if a detainee obtains such evidence, he can request that the Deputy Secretary of Defense convene a new CSRT. Whatever the merits of this procedure, it is an insufficient replacement for the factual review these detainees are entitled to receive through habeas corpus. The Deputy Secretary's determination whether to initiate new proceedings is wholly a discretionary one. And we see no way to construe the DTA to allow a detainee to challenge the Deputy Secretary's decision not to open a new CSRT. . . . The Deputy

Secretary's determination whether to convene a new CSRT is not a "status determination of the Combatant Status Review Tribunal," much less a "final decision" of that body.

We do not imply DTA review would be a constitutionally sufficient replacement for habeas corpus but for these limitations on the detainee's ability to present exculpatory evidence. For even if it were possible, as a textual matter, to read into the statute each of the necessary procedures we have identified, we could not overlook the cumulative effect of our doing so. To hold that the detainees at Guantanamo may, under the DTA, challenge the President's legal authority to detain them, contest the CSRT's findings of fact, supplement the record on review with exculpatory evidence, and request an order of release would come close to reinstating the §2241 habeas corpus process Congress sought to deny them. The language of the statute, read in light of Congress' reasons for enacting it, cannot bear this interpretation. Petitioners have met their burden of establishing that the DTA review process is, on its face, an inadequate substitute for habeas corpus.

Although we do not hold that an adequate substitute must duplicate §2241 in all respects, it suffices that the Government has not established that the detainees' access to the statutory review provisions at issue is an adequate substitute for the writ of habeas corpus. MCA §7 thus effects an unconstitutional suspension of the writ. . . .

Practical Considerations

In light of our conclusion that there is no jurisdictional bar to the District Court's entertaining petitioners' claims the question remains whether there are prudential barriers to habeas corpus review under these circumstances.

The Government argues petitioners must seek review of their CSRT determinations in the Court of Appeals before they can proceed with their habeas corpus actions in the District Court. As noted earlier, in other contexts and for prudential reasons this Court has required exhaustion of alternative remedies before a prisoner can seek federal habeas relief. Most of these cases were brought by prisoners in state custody. . . and thus involved federalism concerns that are not relevant here. But we have extended this rule to require defendants in courts-martial to exhaust their military appeals before proceeding with a federal habeas corpus action.

The real risks, the real threats, of terrorist attacks are constant and not likely soon to abate. The ways to disrupt our life and laws are so many and unforeseen that the Court should not attempt even some general catalogue of crises that might occur. Certain principles are apparent, however. Practical considerations and exigent circumstances inform the definition and reach of the law's writs, including habeas corpus. The cases and our tradition reflect this precept.

In cases involving foreign citizens detained abroad by the Executive, it likely would be both an impractical and unprecedented extension of judicial power to assume that habeas corpus would be available at the moment the prisoner is taken into custody. If and when habeas corpus jurisdiction applies, as it does in these cases, then proper deference can be accorded to reasonable procedures for screening and initial detention under lawful and proper conditions of confinement and treatment for a reasonable period of time. Domestic exigencies, furthermore, might also impose such onerous burdens on the Government that here, too, the Judicial Branch would be required to devise sensible rules for staying habeas corpus proceedings until the Government can comply with its requirements in a responsible way. Here, as is true with detainees apprehended abroad, a relevant consideration in determining the courts' role is whether there are suitable alternative processes in place to protect against the arbitrary exercise of governmental power.

The cases before us, however, do not involve detainees who have been held for a short period of time while awaiting their CSRT determinations. Were that the case, or were it probable that the Court of Appeals could complete a prompt review of their applications, the case for requiring temporary abstention or exhaustion of alternative remedies would be much stronger. These qualifications no longer pertain here. In some of these cases six years have elapsed without the judicial oversight that habeas corpus or an adequate substitute demands. And there has been no showing that the Executive faces such onerous burdens that it cannot respond to habeas corpus actions. To require these detainees to complete DTA review before proceeding with their habeas corpus actions would be to require additional months, if not years, of delay. The first DTA review applications were filed over a year ago, but no decisions on the merits have been issued. While some delay in fashioning new procedures is unavoidable, the costs of delay can no longer be borne by those who are held in custody. The detainees in these cases are entitled to a prompt habeas corpus hearing.

Our decision today holds only that the petitioners before us are entitled to seek the writ; that the DTA review procedures are an inadequate substitute for habeas corpus; and that the petitioners in these cases need not exhaust the review procedures in the Court of Appeals before proceeding with their habeas actions in the District Court. The only law we identify as unconstitutional is MCA §7. Accordingly, both the DTA and the CSRT process remain intact. Our holding with regard to exhaustion should not be read to imply that a habeas court should intervene the moment an enemy combatant steps foot in a territory where the writ runs. The Executive is entitled to a reasonable period of time to determine a detainee's status before a court entertains that detainee's habeas corpus petition. The CSRT process is the mechanism Congress and the President set up to deal with these issues. Except in cases of undue delay, federal courts should refrain from entertaining an enemy combatant's habeas corpus petition at least until after the Department, acting via the CSRT, has had a chance to review his status. . . .

Honoring Freedom's First Principles

In considering both the procedural and substantive standards used to impose detention to prevent acts of terrorism, proper deference must be accorded to the political branches. Unlike the President and some designated Members of Congress, neither the Members of this Court nor most federal judges begin the day with briefings that may describe new and serious threats to our Nation and its people. The law must accord the Executive substantial authority to apprehend and detain those who pose a real danger to our security. . . .

Security depends upon a sophisticated intelligence apparatus and the ability of our Armed Forces to act and to interdict. There are further considerations, however. Security subsists, too, in fidelity to freedom's first principles. Chief among these are freedom from arbitrary and unlawful restraint and the personal liberty that is secured by adherence to the separation of powers. It is from these principles that the judicial authority to consider petitions for habeas corpus relief derives.

Our opinion does not undermine the Executive's powers as Commander in Chief. On the contrary, the exercise of those powers is vindicated, not eroded, when confirmed by the Judicial Branch. Within the Constitution's separation-of-powers structure, few exercises of judicial power are as legitimate or as necessary as the responsibility to hear challenges to the authority of the Executive to imprison a person. Some of these petitioners have been in custody for six years with no definitive judicial determination as to the legality of their detention. Their access to the writ is a necessity to determine the lawfulness of their status, even if, in the end, they do not obtain the relief they seek.

Because our Nation's past military conflicts have been of limited duration, it has been possible to leave the outer boundaries of war powers undefined. If, as some fear, terrorism continues to pose dangerous threats to us for years to come, the Court might not have this luxury. This result is not inevitable, however. The political branches, consistent with their independent obligations to interpret and uphold the Constitution, can engage in a genuine debate about how best to preserve constitutional values while protecting the Nation from terrorism.

It bears repeating that our opinion does not address the content of the law that governs petitioners' detention. That is a matter yet to be determined. We hold that petitioners may invoke the fundamental procedural protections of habeas corpus. The laws and Constitution are designed to survive, and remain in force, in extraordinary times. Liberty and security can be reconciled; and in our system they are reconciled within the framework of the law. The Framers decided that habeas corpus, a right of first importance, must be a part of that framework, a part of that law.

The determination by the Court of Appeals that the Suspension Clause and its protections are inapplicable to petitioners was in error. The judgment of the Court of Appeals is reversed. The cases are remanded to the Court of Appeals with instructions that it remand the cases to the District Court for proceedings consistent with this opinion.

Combatant Status Review Tribunals Are a Sham

Stephen Abraham

*Stephen Abraham is a lawyer who is commissioned as a lieuten-
ant colonel in the U.S. Army Reserve. Since 1982 he has served
as an intelligence officer and was involved with the Combatant
Status Review Tribunals (CSRTs) at the detainee facilities on the
U.S. military base in Guantánamo, Cuba, from September 2004
to March 2005. Abraham supplied the following affidavit to the
defense counsel for Fawzi Khalid Abdullah Fahad, a Guantánamo
detainee who is suing the United States for wrongful imprisonment. In his testimony, Abraham claims that CSRTs are poorly
conducted, lack experienced personnel, and willfully fail to examine evidence that might be used to exonerate detainees and
end their confinement.*

From September 11, 2004, to March 9, 2005, I was on active
duty and assigned to OARDEC [Office for the Administrative Review of the Detention of Enemy Combatants]. Rear
Admiral [James M.] McGarrah served as the Director of OAR-
DEC during the entirety of my assignment.

While assigned to OARDEC, in addition to other duties. I
worked as an agency liaison, responsible for coordinating with
government agencies, including certain Department of De-

Stephen Abraham, "Reply to Opposition to Petition for Rehearing," Khaled A.F. al
Odah Defense Counsel, Petition to the Supreme Court, June 22, 2007.

fense ("DoD") and non-DoD organizations, to gather or validate information relating to detainees for use in CSRTs. I also served as a member of a CSRT, and had the opportunity to observe and participate in the operation of the CSRT process.

Lack of Trained Personnel

As stated in the McGarrah Dec. [Declaration], the information comprising the Government Information and the Government Evidence was not compiled personally by the CSRT Recorder, but by other individuals in OARDEC. The vast majority of the personnel assigned to OARDEC were reserve officers from the different branches of service (Army, Navy, Air Force, Marines) of varying grades and levels of general military experience. Few had any experience or training in the legal or intelligence fields.

The Recorders of the tribunals were typically relatively junior officers with little training or experience in matters relating to the collection, processing, analyzing, and/or dissemination of intelligence material, In no instances known to me did any of the Recorders have any significant personal experience in the field of military intelligence. Similarly, I was unaware of any Recorder having any significant or relevant experience dealing with the agencies providing information to be used as a part of the CSRT process.

The Recorders exercised little control over the process of accumulating information to be presented to the CSRT board members. Rather, the information was typically aggregated by individuals identified as case writers who, in most instances, had the same limited degree of knowledge and experience relating to the intelligence community and intelligence products. The case writers, and not the Recorders, were primarily responsible for accumulating documents, including assembling documents to be used in the drafting of an unclassified summary of the factual basis for the detainee's designation as an enemy combatant.

Suspect Sources of CSRT Evidence

The information used to prepare the files to be used by the Recorders frequently consisted of finished intelligence products of a generalized nature—often outdated, often "generic," rarely specifically relating to the individual subjects of the CS-RTs or to the circumstances related to those individuals' status.

Beyond "generic" information, the case writer would frequently rely upon information contained within the Joint Detainee Information Management System ("JDIMS"). The subset of that system available to the case writers was limited in terms of the scope of information, typically excluding information that was characterized as highly sensitive law enforcement information, highly classified information, or information not voluntarily released by the originating agency. In that regard, JDIMS did not constitute a complete repository, although this limitation was frequently not understood by individuals with access to or who relied upon the system as a source of information. Other databases available to the case writer were similarly deficient. The case writers and Recorders did not have access to numerous information sources generally available within the intelligence community.

As one of only a few intelligence-trained and suitably cleared officers, I served as a liaison while assigned to OAR-DEC, acting as a go-between for OARDEC and various intelligence organizations. In that capacity, I was tasked to review and/or obtain information relating to individual subjects of the CSRTs. More specifically, I was asked to confirm and represent in a statement to be relied upon by the CSRT board members that the organizations did not possess "exculpatory information" [i.e., information that could clear the defendant of guilt] relating to the subject of the CSRT.

Limited Access to Information

During my trips to the participating organizations, I was allowed only limited access to information, typically prescreened and filtered. I was not permitted to see any information other than that specifically prepared in advance of my visit. I was not permitted to request that further searches be performed. I was given no assurances that the information provided for my examination represented a complete compilation of information or that any summary of information constituted an accurate distillation of the body of available information relating to the subject.

I was specifically told on a number of occasions that the information provided to me was all that I would be shown, but I was never told that the information that was provided constituted all available information. On those occasions when I asked that a representative of the organization provide a written statement that there was no exculpatory evidence, the requests were summarily denied.

Further Access Denied

At one point, following a review of information, I asked the Office of General Counsel of the intelligence organization that I was visiting for a statement that no exculpatory information had been withheld. I explained that I was tasked to review all available materials and to reach a conclusion regarding the non-existence of exculpatory information, and that I could not do so without knowing that I had seen all information.

The request was denied, coupled with a refusal even to acknowledge whether there existed additional information that I was not permitted to review. In short, based upon the selective review that I was permitted, I was left to "infer" from the absence of exculpatory information in the materials I was allowed to review that no such information existed in materials I was not allowed to review.

Following that exchange, I communicated to Rear Admiral McGarrah and the OARDEC Deputy Director the fundamental limitations imposed upon my review of the organization's files and my inability to state conclusively that no exculpatory information existed relating to the CSRT subjects. It was not possible for me to certify or validate the non-existence of exculpatory evidence as related to any individual undergoing the CSRT process.

The content of intelligence products, including databases, made available to case writers, Recorders, or liaison officers, was often left entirely to the discretion of the organizations providing the information. What information was not included in the bodies of intelligence products was typically unknown to the case writers and Recorders, as was the basis for limiting the information. In other words, the person preparing materials for use by the CSRT board members did not know whether they had examined all available information or even why they possessed some pieces of information but not others.

A Lack of Context

Although OARDEC personnel often received large amounts of information, they often had no context for determining whether the information was relevant or probative and no basis for determining what additional information would be necessary to establish a basis for determining the reasonableness of any matter to be offered to the CSRT board members. Often, information that was gathered was discarded by the case writer or the Recorder because it was considered to be ambiguous, confusing, or poorly written. Such a determination was frequently the result of the case writer or Recorder's lack of training or experience with the types of information provided. In my observation, the case writer or Recorder, without proper experience or a basis for giving context to information, often rejected some information arbitrarily while accepting other information without any articulable rationale.

The case writer's summaries were reviewed for quality assurance, a process that principally focused on format and grammar. The quality assurance review would not ordinarily check the accuracy of the information underlying the case writer's unclassified summary for the reason that the quality assurance reviewer typically had little more experience than the case writer and, again, no relevant or meaningful intelligence or legal experience, and therefore had no skills by which to critically assess the substantive portions of the summaries.

Following the quality assurance process, the unclassified summary and the information assembled by the case writer in support of the summary would then be forwarded to the Recorder. It was very rare that a Recorder or a personal representative would seek additional information beyond that information provided by the case writer.

Favorable Findings Is Frowned Upon

It was not apparent to me how assignments to CSRT panels were made, nor was I personally involved in that process. Nevertheless, I discerned the determinations of who would be assigned to any particular position, whether as a member of a CSRT or to some other position, to be largely the product of ad hoc decisions by a relatively small group of individuals. All CSRT panel members were assigned to OARDEC and reported ultimately to Rear Admiral McGarrah. It was well known by the officers in OARDEC that any time a CSRT panel determined that a detainee was not properly classified as an enemy combatant, the panel members would have to explain their finding to the OARDEC Deputy Director. There would be intensive scrutiny of the finding by Rear Admiral McGarrah who would, in turn, have to explain the finding to his superiors, including the Under Secretary of the Navy.

On one occasion, I was assigned to a CSRT panel with two other officers, an Air Force colonel and an Air Force major, the latter understood by me to be a judge advocate. We reviewed evidence presented to us regarding the recommended status of a detainee. All of us found the information presented to lack substance.

What were purported to be specific statements of fact lacked even the most fundamental earmarks of objectively credible evidence. Statements allegedly made by percipient witnesses lacked detail. Reports presented generalized statements in indirect and passive forms without stating the source of the information or providing a basis for establishing the reliability or the credibility of the source. Statements of interrogators presented to the panel offered inferences from which we were expected to draw conclusions favoring a finding of "enemy combatant" but that, upon even limited questioning from the panel, yielded the response from the Recorder, "We'll have to get back to you." The personal representative did not participate in any meaningful way.

On the basis of the paucity and weakness of the information provided both during and after the CSRT hearing, we determined that there was no factual basis for concluding that the individual should be classified as an enemy combatant. Rear Admiral McGarrah and the Deputy Director immediately questioned the validity of our findings. They directed us to write out the specific questions that we had raised concerning the evidence to allow the Recorder an opportunity to provide further responses. We were then ordered to reopen the hearing to allow the Recorder to present further argument as to why the detainee should be classified as an enemy combatant. Ultimately, in the absence of any substantive response to the questions and no basis for concluding that additional information would be forthcoming, we did not change our determination that the detainee was not properly classified as an enemy combatant. OARDEC's response to the outcome was consistent with the few other instances in which a finding of "Not an Enemy Combatant" (NEC) had been reached by CSRT boards. In each of the meetings that I attended with OARDEC leadership following a finding of NEC, the focus of inquiry on the part of the leadership was "what went wrong,"

I was not assigned to another CSRT panel.

> *"Properly understood, the Suspension Clause operates as a direct restraint on the government regardless of where any particular habeas petitioner is detained."*

Detained Enemy Combatants Have a Right to Habeas Corpus

American Civil Liberties Union and Public Justice

In the following statement in support of the petitioners in the Boumediene v. Bush *and* Al Odah v. United States *U.S. Supreme Court cases, the American Civil Liberties Union (ACLU) and Public Justice assert that the decision of the U.S. court of appeals regarding these cases should be overturned. The appellate court ruled in 2006 that the right to challenge imprisonment based on the writ of habeas corpus does not apply to enemy combatant detainees at Guantánamo Naval Base. The ACLU and Public Justice insist that due process as guaranteed by the Constitution should apply to all persons who are detained by agents of the U.S. government unless the specific case proves that securing these rights would be either "impracticable or anomalous" as Justice John Harlan previously concluded in* Reid v. Covert *(1957). The ACLU and Public Justice state that this conclusion was already drawn in the 2004 case* Rasul v. Bush *in which the Court acknowledged that Guantánamo detainees could pursue constitutional claims against the government through habeas corpus petitions. Therefore, the Court should again rule that the petitioners in these cases have the right to know the charges against them and to question their detention. The ACLU is a nonprofit legal defense organization devoted to protecting the rights guaranteed by the Constitution. Public Justice is a public interest law firm.*

This case represents the latest stage in the government's on-going effort to avoid any meaningful judicial review of its decision to hold hundreds of detainees without charges or trial at the U.S. Naval Base at Guantanamo Bay for as long as it chooses. The government is unapologetic about its position. In the government's view, its detention policies at Guantanamo Bay are not subject to any legal constraint beyond the plainly inadequate safeguards that Congress has belatedly enacted, for two simple reasons: the detainees are not U.S. citizens and they are imprisoned outside the United States.

For nearly eight centuries, the writ of habeas corpus has served as a check against arbitrary executive detention. The Framers regarded habeas corpus as so essential to ordered liberty that they included a provision in the Constitution providing that "the privilege of the writ of habeas corpus shall not be suspended, unless when in cases of rebellion or invasion the public safety may require it." U.S. Const. art. I, § 9, cl. 2. The government does not argue that those conditions have been met. Instead, the government argues, and the Court of Appeals agreed, that "the Constitution does not confer rights on aliens without property or presence within the United States." *Boumediene v. Bush* (D.C. Cir. 2007).

This Court has rejected such a categorical rule for more than a hundred years. In different decisions, the Court has emphasized different factors in determining whether the Constitution applies. Here, however, every standard that the Court has articulated is easily satisfied. First, petitioners are asserting fundamental rights. Second, the U.S. has exercised exclusive jurisdiction and control over Guantanamo Bay since 1903. Third, applying the Constitution to these facts would not be "impracticable and anomalous." Indeed, the constitutional anomaly in this case has been created by the decision, which allows the government to act with impunity and outside any system of checks and balances.

Because it represents such a departure from this Court's longstanding jurisprudence, the decision can and should be reversed on multiple grounds. Properly understood, the Suspension Clause operates as a direct restraint on the government regardless of where any particular habeas petitioner is detained. The alternative procedures established by Congress in the Military Commissions Act are a patently inadequate substitute for habeas corpus. Respondents' actions in this case are subject to constitutional scrutiny because of the special status of Guantanamo Bay. And, regardless of whether the Constitution applies in its entirety at Guantanamo Bay, Petitioners are entitled to invoke the Suspension and Due Process Clauses because both provisions protect fundamental rights.

Rather than repeat these arguments, each of which is discussed at length by petitioners and other *amici*, this brief focuses on the "impracticable and anomalous" test first articulated by Justice Harlan in 1957, elaborated upon by Justice [Anthony] Kennedy in 1990, and implicitly endorsed by a majority of this Court in 2004. . . .

The Court of Appeals Erred

The Court of Appeals erroneously interpreted this Court's precedents in stating that "the Constitution does not confer rights on aliens without property or presence within the United States." For at least 100 years, this Court has rejected such categorical pronouncements in deciding whether the U.S. government is subject to constitutional constraints outside the United States. Rather, when confronted with claims of constitutional violations outside the United States, this Court has examined the particular circumstances of each case and reached various conclusions as to whether and how the U.S.

Constitution applies. Beginning with the Insular Cases of the early twentieth century, the Court has evaluated many relevant factors, such as the nature of the right, the context in which the right is asserted, the nationality of the person asserting the right, and whether recognition of the right would conflict with any foreign sovereign's laws or customs. That case-by-case evaluation belies the Court of Appeals' categorical holding that the Constitution can never constrain the government's conduct with respect to a non-U.S. citizen without property or presence within the United States. . . .

The "Impracticable and Anomalous" Test

Although this Court long ago concluded that constitutional claims arising outside the United States must be evaluated on a case-by-case basis, its decisions in this area "have been neither unambiguous nor uniform," as the Court itself has acknowledged. That ambiguity may not matter in this case because Petitioners are entitled to prevail under the fundamental rights doctrine of the Insular Cases, standing alone. Nevertheless, this case provides the Court with an opportunity to bring important clarity to the law by applying the "impracticable and anomalous" test to its consideration of Petitioners' constitutional claims.

The decision is not the first by the D.C. Circuit misinterpreting this Court's precedents and stating that non-citizens outside the United States do not have any constitutional rights. . . . The Court should make a clear statement to prevent the lower courts from adopting such categorical rules with unforeseeable future consequences.

The "impracticable and anomalous" test was first articulated by Justice Harlan in his concurring opinion in *Reid v. Covert*, 354 U.S. 1. Like the plurality, . . . Justice Harlan expressly rejected a categorical rule that the Constitution should never apply to the trial of U.S. citizens outside the United States. In his view, the question whether any asserted constitutional right applies outside the United States should depend upon an analysis of the particular circumstances of the case:

> [I]t seems to me that the basic teaching of *Ross* [*v. McIntyre*, 1891] and the Insular Cases is that there is no rigid and abstract rule that Congress, as a condition precedent to exercising power over Americans overseas, must exercise it subject to all the guarantees of the Constitution, no matter what the conditions and considerations are that would make adherence to a specific guarantee altogether impracticable and anomalous. . . . Decision is easy if one adopts the constricting view that these constitutional guarantees as a totality do or do not 'apply' overseas. But, for me, the question is which guarantees of the Constitution should apply in view of the particular circumstances, the practical necessities, and the possible alternatives which Congress had before it. The question is one of judgment, not compulsion.

Thus, Justice Harlan put into words what the plurality did in fact—examine all the relevant circumstances before drawing a conclusion about whether a constitutional right applies in the given circumstance.

Although the particular facts of *Reid* involved U.S. citizens in foreign countries, Justice Harlan's "impracticable and anomalous" test has not been limited to claims by U.S. citizens. Justice Kennedy subsequently adopted and refined Justice Harlan's "impracticable and anomalous" test in *United States v. Verdugo-Urquidez*, which involved a constitutional claim by a Mexican citizen based on events arising in Mexico. Justice Kennedy began his concurring opinion in *Verdugo-Urquidez* by noting that "the Government may act only as the Constitution authorizes, whether the actions in question are foreign or domestic." But, he concluded, "[t]he conditions and considerations of this case would make adherence to the Fourth Amendment's warrant requirement impracticable and anomalous," based on various practical factors such as "[t]he absence of local judges or magistrates available to issue warrants." Notwithstanding this conclusion, Justice Kennedy did not treat the "impracticable and anomalous" test as limited to the particular circumstances of *Reid*—*i.e.*, a constitutional claim by a U.S. citizen abroad. As he explained in *Verdugo-Urquidez*: "The restrictions that the United States must observe with reference to aliens beyond its territory or jurisdiction depend . . . on general principles of interpretation, not on an inquiry as to who formed the Constitution or a construction that some rights are mentioned as being those of 'the people.'"

In one of its first cases implicating national security after September 11, 2001, a majority of this Court appeared to approve the Harlan-Kennedy "impracticable and anomalous" test. In *Rasul v. Bush*, 542 U.S. 466 (2004), the Court held that non-citizens detained by the United States at the U.S. navy base at Guanatanamo Bay had the right to pursue constitutional and statutory claims against the U.S. government through habeas petitions under 28 U.S.C. § 2241, 542 U.S. at 484. Although the Court's holding concerned statutory jurisdiction, the Court considered in a footnote whether the Guantanamo detainees in *Rasul* had alleged "custody in violation of the Constitution or laws or treaties of the United States," as required for jurisdiction under 28 U.S.C. § 2241(c)(3). The Court concluded that the detainees' allegations—of prolonged executive detention without access to counsel and without being charged with any wrongdoing—"unquestionably describe 'custody in violation of the Constitution or laws or treaties of the United States.'" 542 U.S. at 484 n.15. Immediately following this statement, the Court cited the portion of Justice Kennedy's *Verdugo-Urquidez* concurrence that set forth the "impracticable and anomalous" test and also the "cases cited therein." The Court of Appeals sought to minimize the significance of that footnote in *Rasul* by dismissing it as dicta [extraneous opinions]. Whether dicta or not, this Court's observation in *Rasul* was fundamentally sound and should now be reaffirmed.

By adopting the "impracticable and anomalous" test, the Court would provide much-needed guidance to the lower courts in an age of increasing U.S. government activity outside the 50 states. The test permits courts to account for different conditions and locations, from sovereign foreign countries (as in *Reid* and *Verdugo-Urquidez*) to unusual leaseholds such as the U.S. Naval Base at Guantanamo Bay. The "impracticable and anomalous" test also strikes the proper balance between the Constitution's structure of limited government power, and the need of the U.S. government to act effectively in the global arena. By applying the test, U.S. courts can give due recognition to core constitutional rights—such as the right against indefinite executive detention without any charge and based on evidence obtained by torture—while abiding by the common-sense principle that not every person outside the United States may enjoy the full panoply of rights under the Constitution when he encounters an agent of the U.S. government.

Petitioners Have Asserted Valid Claims

The validity of Petitioners' constitutional claims has been amply demonstrated in Petitioners' own briefs and in the briefs submitted by other *amici*. We will not repeat those arguments here. For present purposes, we note that if the Court does adopt the "impracticable and anomalous" test, Petitioners' constitutional claims are more than sufficient to meet that test. In a nation committed to the rule of law, it would be "impracticable and anomalous" to rule that Petitioners have no right to challenge their detention in federal court after they have been held without charges or trials, in some instances, for more than five years. . . .

On the facts of this case, it would plainly be neither "impracticable" nor "anomalous" to recognize the constitutional rights that Petitioners assert. First, by challenging their indefinite detention by the Executive Branch without any charges or trial, Petitioners raise claims that lie at the very heart of the Bill of Rights and the Suspension Clause. Accordingly, this case falls squarely within the longstanding fundamental rights doctrine from the Insular Cases. Under the Insular Cases, this alone is enough to require reversal of the decision.

Second, there are no practical impediments, nor any risk of conflict between sovereign nations, in recognizing Petitioners' rights under the Fifth Amendment and the Suspension Clause. The petitioners are detained not in a sovereign foreign nation, but at the U.S. Naval Base in Guantanamo, which this Court has already held to be unique because the United States has "plenary and exclusive jurisdiction." Thus, there is no risk of any conflict between the rights under the Constitution that the Petitioners assert and foreign laws. Nor would recognition of Petitioners' rights in habeas corpus present undue logistical difficulties.

Based on all the circumstances, it would not be "impracticable and anomalous" to hold that core due process rights against indefinite executive detention apply at Guantanamo or to recognize Petitioners' access to the courts under the Suspension Clause. This Court has already implicitly taken that view in *Rasul*, and should make that holding explicit here.

Enemy Aliens Have Never Had the Right to Habeas Corpus

Criminal Justice Legal Foundation

The Criminal Justice Legal Foundation (CJLF) is a public interest law firm that is noted for winning more cases before the U.S. Supreme Court in recent decades than any other public interest organization. In the following opinion brief in support of the government in the Supreme Court cases Boumediene v. Bush *and* Al Odah v. United States, *the CJLF contends that neither the petitioners nor any of the detainees held at Guantánamo Bay Naval Base have the right to challenge their detention through the U.S. courts. According to the CJLF, there is no judicial precedent for granting enemy aliens the writ of habeas corpus to question their imprisonment. Indeed, the CJLF states that amendments to the habeas corpus statute in 2005 have definitively removed this remedy from the detainees captured during the war on terror. Furthermore, the CJLF maintains that only Congress can alter this decision; the courts have no authority to define the laws of the land or determine national security policy.*

The "privilege of the writ of habeas corpus" protected by the Suspension Clause [of the U.S. Constitution] is limited to people who are part of the population of the United States. . . . That term is broader than just citizens; it includes

Criminal Justice Legal Foundation, "Amicus curiae in support of respondents" *Boumediene v. Bush* and *al Odah v. United States*, October 2007. Reproduced by permission.

resident aliens and even visitors. However, it is not so broad as to include persons who had never entered the United States or any area under its control prior to being brought in as military prisoners.

None of the historical cases cited by petitioners or supporting *amici* ["friends of the court"] extended the writ to anyone in petitioners' status. . . .

Unlike the Court's prior detainee cases, this case involves an unambiguous repeal of habeas jurisdiction by Congress, expressly applicable to this case. Petitioners are therefore asking the judicial branch to overrule a joint decision of both of the political branches on a question of foreign and military policy. The judiciary is not the proper forum for such issues. The detainees' remedies are those Congress has provided plus the diplomatic efforts of their home countries. . . .

Habeas Corpus Has Been Suspended

Article I, § 9, cl. 2, of the Constitution provides, "The Privilege of the Writ of Habeas Corpus shall not be suspended, unless when in Cases of Rebellion or Invasion the public Safety may require it." Petitioners argue that the Suspension Clause limits Congress's ability to suspend their privilege to habeas corpus. This argument depends on the premise that petitioners are holders of the "privilege" referred to in the Suspension Clause. They are not.

"It is the holdings of our cases, rather than their dicta, [explanatory or editorial statements] that we must attend. . . ." *Kokkonen v. Guardian Life Ins. Co.* (1994). The question presented in *Rasul v. Bush* (2004),[1] and hence the holding of the case, concerned the scope of the habeas statute as it then read. The statute at that time made no distinction between citizens and aliens. The discussion of the rights of aliens to habeas review at common law is dictum.

1. In *Rasul v. Bush* the Supreme Court asserted that the courts did have the authority to hear wrongful imprisonment cases brought against the government by detainees at Guantánamo Bay Naval Base.

As subsequently amended [in 2005 by an amendment proposed by Senator Lindsey Graham], 28 U. S. C. § 2241 now distinguishes between aliens detained as enemy combatants and other persons. Unlike the previous, short-lived amendments of Public Law 109-148, § 1005(e)(1), 119 Stat. 2742, and Public Law 109-163, § 1405(e)(1), 119 Stat. 3477, the current habeas statute does not distinguish cases according to the place of detention. The question of whether the amended habeas statute violates the Suspension Clause should therefore begin with the distinction drawn by Congress based on the status of the alien, not the distinction based on the location of detention that is the primary basis of the Court of Appeals' opinion.

Status More Important than Location

Discussions of the history of the writ often conflate issues of territorial reach with issues of the petitioner's status. . . .

The privilege of habeas corpus was meant only to protect those who were "part of [the] population." *The Japanese Immigrant Case*, (1903). Aliens detained as enemy combatants, arrested overseas and detained by the military on a military base, have never become part of the population. They would not be part of the population regardless of whether they were detained in Guantanamo Bay, South Carolina, or Afghanistan. In *Hamdi v. Rumsfeld*, (2004), concerning the review available to a citizen detainee, the plurality said, "It is not at all clear why [place of detention] should make a determinative constitutional difference." There is also no good reason why it should make such a difference in the case of aliens who are not part of the population.

Petitioners as Population Members

The fact that the United States has generously extended constitutional protection to aliens living within the country, to visitors, and even to those who enter illegally, does not support a conclusion that we must extend the full panoply of constitutional rights to every alien who happens to be on territory in the control of our government. The government's ability to grant or deny a right depends on whom that right was placed in the Constitution to protect. History shows that the purpose of the Suspension Clause was to protect the people of the United States.

[*Johnson v.*] *Eisentrager* rejected a claim of a constitutional right to habeas corpus by enemy aliens. While the *Eisentrager* decision emphasized the fact that the enemy aliens were outside the United States, it did not address the territorial application of habeas corpus alone. The Court also noted, "The alien, to whom the United States has been traditionally hospitable, has been accorded a generous and ascending scale of rights as he increases his identity with our society." The question is where the petitioners are on that scale and where one must be to hold the privilege of the writ of habeas corpus.

In *The Japanese Immigrant Case*, the petitioner was "an alien, who has entered the country, and has become subject in all respects to its jurisdiction, *and a part of its population*, although alleged to be illegally here...." 189 U. S., at 101 (emphasis added). Thus, although Ms. Yamataya, the alien subject to deportation in *The Japanese Immigrant Case*, had been in the United States for less than two weeks; she was entitled to basic due process. Aliens outside the population are not entitled to basic due process. Such aliens are only afforded the process Congress has provided to them. Thus, a would-be immigrant "on the threshold of initial entry stands on a different footing" even when he was within the territorial boundaries of the United States (Ellis Island) and deprived of his liberty by agents of the federal government.

The Limits of Legal Precedents

Petitioners argue that they have a constitutional right to habeas corpus as it existed in 1789. They base their claim on this

Court's ruling in *INS v. St. Cyr*, (2001). *St. Cyr* indicates that "at the absolute minimum, the Suspension Clause protects the writ 'as it existed in 1789.'" However, this right exists only for those who were "part of its population" . . . and who were detained under federal law. English decisions from the time of the Founding and earlier, as well as early American decisions, clarify the limits of constitutional protection. At best, habeas corpus "'as it existed in 1789'" extended to territories and not to aliens who were not a "part of its population."

In *St. Cyr*, this Court upheld the authority of federal courts to grant a writ of habeas corpus to an alien who had been "admitted to the United States *as a lawful permanent resident* in 1986." (emphasis added). The Court granted St. Cyr's petition to review the legal question of whether discretionary deportation relief under Illegal Immigration Reform and Immigrant Responsibility Act of 1996 (IIRIRA) and the Antiterrorism and Effective Death Penalty Act of 1996 (AEDPA) could apply to an alien who had pled guilty to a deportable crime before either IIRIRA or the AEDPA had been enacted. While this Court recognized that the case had the potential to raise the question "of what the Suspension Clause protects," this Court declined to address the constitutional issue. To inform its statutory interpretation, the Court examined the historical exercise of habeas jurisdiction in England and the United States. In its analysis, this Court found that "[i]n England prior to 1789, in the Colonies and in this Nation during the formative years of our Government, the writ of habeas corpus was available to *nonenemy* aliens as well as to citizens." (emphasis added). . . .

Courts Cannot Contravene Statute

The present case comes to the Court in a very different posture regarding separation of powers than the previous cases. In *Rasul v. Bush*, (2004), and *Hamdan v. Rumsfeld*, (2006), there was room for doubt on interpretation of the pertinent

Acts of Congress. In the present case, there is no doubt. The statutory language is as clear as words can be that Congress repealed habeas jurisdiction for these petitioners and that the repeal applies to pending cases. The Court of Appeals aptly characterized the argument to the contrary as "nonsense."

In the previous cases, this Court determined that executive decisions regarding the conduct of the war on terror were contrary to the law enacted by Congress. In this case, petitioners ask the Court to overrule a joint decision of the executive and legislative branches. That is a far different matter. Whatever the relative roles of the executive and legislative branches in foreign policy may be, the role of the judiciary is minimal. This primacy of the political branches extends to the treatment of aliens.

Certainly questions can be raised about the wisdom of current policies. The proper balance between security needs and America's relations with other countries and reputation in the world is debatable. But a court of law is not the forum for that debate. We are in a new kind of war, with a new kind of danger and a new kind of enemy. The proper response and the correct balance are political decisions for the political branches to make.

Where the statute is clear, the only justifiable question is whether it violates a permanent principle that the people have placed in the Constitution. Petitioners in this case are not holders of the "privilege of the writ of habeas corpus," U.S. Const., Art. I, § 9, cl. 2, as that privilege was understood by the people when they ratified that limit on congressional authority. The statute is not unconstitutional as applied to them. Their remedies are the reviews provided in the statutes and the diplomatic efforts of their home countries.

Organizations to Contact

The editors have compiled the following list of organizations concerned with the issues presented in this book. The descriptions are derived from materials provided by the organizations. All have publications or information available for interested readers. The list was compiled on the date of publication of the present volume; the information provided here may change. Be aware that many organizations take several weeks or longer to respond to inquiries, so allow as much time as possible.

American Civil Liberties Union (ACLU)
125 Broad St., 18th Fl., New York, NY   10004
Web site: www.aclu.org

The ACLU coordinates national campaigns through regional offices to protect the rights and liberties guaranteed by the Bill of Rights in the U.S. Constitution. The organization focuses on issues ranging from the death penalty to free speech and from the rights of the poor to national security. Recently the ACLU began the "Close Guantánamo" Campaign, seeking to shut down the military detention facility in Cuba where most terrorist suspects and enemy combatants are being held. Specifically, the neglect of providing due process for detainees, absence of trials, and reports of torture form the grounds for the ACLU's demand that Guantánamo be closed. Numerous reports detailing the ACLU's positions and recommended actions concerning Guantánamo and other terrorism- and national security–related issues are available on the organization's Web site.

American Enterprise Institute (AEI)
1150 Seventeenth St. NW, Washington, DC   20036
(202) 862-5800 • fax: (202) 862-7177
Web site: www.aei.org

AEI, a conservative think tank, has worked since 1943 to promote conservative values such as limited government, a free-market economy, and a strong national defense in all American public policies. Regarding the detention and prosecution of enemy combatants and suspected terrorists, AEI has sponsored conferences providing a forum for discussion of pertinent issues such as the writ of habeas corpus and has also published numerous reports outlining its stance on such topics. The *American* is the institute's bimonthly magazine that provides conservative viewpoints on current topics.

Cato Institute
1000 Massachusetts Ave. NW, Washington, DC   20001
(202) 842-0200 • fax: (202) 842-3490
Web site: www.cato.org

The Cato Institute is a libertarian think tank providing public policy research promoting ideas such as individual liberty, limited government, and the rule of law. Regarding national security, the organization encourages strategic independence and use of military force only in situations where America is directly threatened. In reports, congressional testimony, and the filing of amicus briefs, Cato has weighed in on issues such as detainment of enemy combatants and use of military tribunals as a means of prosecuting terrorist suspects. Many of these documents are available on its Web site.

Center for Constitutional Rights (CCR)
666 Broadway, 7th Fl., New York, NY   10012
(212) 614-6464
Web site: www.ccrjustice.org

Since 1966, CCR has actively worked, using litigation, educational outreach, and grassroots coalitions, to ensure that all individuals receive the full protection of rights provided by the U.S. Constitution and the UN Universal Declaration of Human Rights. Some of the current issues receiving attention from this organization include the illegal detention of both citizens and noncitizens at Guantánamo Bay, the government's abuse of power, and the incorporation of international law into the U.S. justice system. CCR has participated in litigation involving trials concerning terrorist suspects and enemy combatants, such as *al Odah v. United States, Hamdan v. Rumsfeld, Hamdi v. Rumsfeld*, and *Rasul v. Bush*. The CCR Web site provides fact sheets on these cases and others, the monthly *Guantánamo Newsletter*, and reports such as "The Military Commissions Act of 2006," and "Faces of Guantánamo."

Center for National Security Studies (CNSS)
1120 Nineteenth St. NW, 8th Fl., Washington, DC   20036
(202) 721-5650 • fax: (202) 530-0128
e-mail: cnss@cnss.org
Web site: www.cnss.org

CNSS is dedicated to ensuring that civil liberties are not curtailed or revoked in the name of increasing national security. Current focuses of the center include the rights of enemy combatants and the legality of military commissions to try terrorist suspects. CNSS filed amicus briefs on behalf of José Padilla, Zacarias Moussaoui, and Salim Ahmed Hamdan, all individuals detained by the U.S. government on enemy combatant charges or in direct association with terrorist activities. Additionally, reports and fact sheets on issues relating to the preservation of rights in the face of national security measures can be found on the CNSS Web site.

Council on Foreign Relations
58 E. Sixty-eighth St., New York, NY   10065
(212) 434-9400 • fax: (212) 434-9800
Web site: www.cfr.org

The Council on Foreign Relations works to promote an increased understanding of the impact of foreign policy choices, by both the United States and other countries, on the global community. The council provides information as well as forums for discussion through the publication of books and the periodical *Foreign Affairs*; sponsorship of meetings for scholars, U.S. politicians, and global leaders; and funding of research and reports on current foreign policies affecting the world. Homeland security and defense, international peace and security, and terrorism are all topics of concern to the organization. Scholars within the organization have written extensively on the detention of enemy combatants, the use of military tribunals to prosecute suspected terrorists, and issues related to the Guantánamo Bay detention center in Cuba. These reports can be found on the organization's Web site.

The Heritage Foundation

214 Massachusetts Ave. NE, Washington, DC   20002
(202) 546-4400 • fax: (202) 546-8328
e-mail: info@heritage.org
Web site: www.heritage.org

The Heritage Foundation is an organization that conducts public policy research adhering to and promoting traditional conservative values. As such, the foundation believes in a strong national defense policy and supports government detention of suspected terrorists and building a military that is armed, capable, and empowered with needed government support to protect American citizens and beliefs on U.S. soil and abroad. The Heritage Foundation operates the Web site NationalSecurity.org which provides current information on the state of U.S. security and publishes numerous reports such as "Treatment of Detainees and Unlawful Combatants: Selected Writings on Guantanamo Bay" and "The War on Terrorism: Habeas Corpus On and Off the Battlefield," detailing its positions on issues relating to the detainment and trial of terrorist suspects.

U.S. Department of Justice (DOJ)

950 Pennsylvania Ave. NW, Washington, DC   20530
(202) 514-2000
e-mail: askdoj@usdoj.gov
Web site: www.usdoj.gov

The DOJ is the cabinet-level office of the U.S. government charged with upholding the laws of the United States in order to protect the country as a whole, as well as all American citizens. Additionally, the department is responsible for ensuring that all Americans receive fair and impartial judgment according to the guarantees of the Constitution. Within the DOJ, Joint Terrorism Task Forces (JTTFs) work both on a local level and in connection with the FBI to ensure that terrorism does not proliferate within individual communities in the United States. Further information on the activities of both the JTTFs and the DOJ as a whole are available on the department's Web site.

For Further Research

Books

Peter Berkowitz, ed., *Terrorism, the Laws of War, and the Constitution: Debating the Enemy Combatant Cases.* Stanford, CA: Hoover Institution Press, 2005.

Clark Butler, ed., *Guantanamo Bay and the Judicial-Moral Treatment of the Other.* West Lafayette, IN: Purdue University Press, 2007.

Elaine Cassel, *The War on Civil Liberties: How Bush and Ashcroft Have Dismantled the Bill of Rights.* Chicago: Lawrence Hill, 2004.

David B. Cohen and John W. Wells, eds., *American National Security and Civil Liberties in an Era of Terrorism.* New York: Palgrave Macmillan, 2004.

Katherine C. Donahue, *Slave of Allah: Zacarias Moussaoui vs. the USA.* Ann Arbor, MI: Pluto, 2007.

Louis Fisher, *Military Tribunals and Presidential Power: American Revolution to the War on Terrorism.* Lawrence: University Press of Kansas, 2005.

Mark S. Hamm, *Terrorism as Crime: From Oklahoma City to al-Qaeda and Beyond.* New York: New York University Press, 2007.

Bruce Hoffman, *Inside Terrorism.* New York: Columbia University Press, 2006.

Peter Latham and Patricia Latham, *Terrorism and the Law: Bringing Terrorists to Justice.* Washington, DC: JKL Communications, 2002.

Richard C. Leone and Greg Anrig Jr., eds., *The War on Our Freedoms: Civil Liberties in an Age of Terrorism.* New York: Public Affairs, 2003.

Joseph Margulies, *Guantanamo and the Abuse of Presidential Power*. New York: Simon & Schuster, 2006.

Abd Samad Moussaoui with Florence Bouquillat, *Zacarias, My Brother: The Making of a Terrorist*. Trans. Simon Pleasance and Fronza Woods. New York: Seven Stories, 2003.

Tram Nguyen, *We Are All Suspects Now: Untold Stories from Immigrant Communities After 9/11*. Boston: Beacon, 2005.

Richard Pildes, ed., *The Constitution in Wartime: Beyond Alarmism and Complacency*. Durham, NC: Duke University Press, 2005.

Richard A. Posner, *Not a Suicide Pact: The Constitution in a Time of National Emergency*. New York: Oxford University Press, 2006.

Robert E. Precht, *Defending Mohammad: Justice on Trial*. Ithaca, NY: Cornell University Press, 2003.

Clive Stafford Smith, *Bad Men: Guantanamo Bay and the Secret Prisons*. London: Weidenfeld & Nicolson, 2007.

Periodicals

General Articles on Terrorism

CQ Researcher "Background: Post-9/11 Whistleblowing," March 31, 2006.

Mitch Frank, "Terror Goes on Trial," *Time*, March 7, 2005.

Michael Greenberger, "Is Criminal Justice a Casualty of the Bush Administration's 'War on Terror'?" *Human Rights*, Winter 2004.

Tony Locy, "The Trials of al Qaeda: Federal Court vs. Military Commission," *Case Western Reserve Journal of International Law*, Spring 2004.

Jeffrey Rosen, "Prevent Defense," *New Republic*, September 6, 2004.

Philip Shenon, "Justice Dept. Must Clarify Role in Inquiry," *New York Times*, May 15, 2004.

Wall Street Journal, "Terrorism on Trial," April 1, 2006.

Benjamin Wittes, "Justice Delayed," *Atlantic Monthly*, March 2006.

The United States of America v. Zacarias Moussaoui

Edward A. Adams, "*Moussaoui v. The United States*," *ABA Journal*, September 2007.

Commonweal, "The Wrong Punishment," April 21, 2006.

Economist, "The One Who Got Away," May 6, 2006.

Adam Liptak, "*Moussaoui* Verdict Highlights Where Juries Fear to Tread," *New York Times*, May 5, 2006.

Michelle Malkin, "Cry No Tears for Terrorists," *Human Events*, April 24, 2006.

Thomas Michael McDonnell, "The Death Penalty: An Obstacle to the 'War Against Terrorism,'" *Vanderbilt Journal of Transnational Law*, March 2004.

Jeff A. Taylor, "How the FBI Let 9/11 Happen," *Reason*, June 2006.

Wall Street Journal, "The Meaning of *Moussaoui*," April 14, 2006.

Hamdi v. Rumsfeld

Bruce Ackerman, "States of Emergency," *American Prospect*, September 2004.

Erwin Chemerinsky, "Three Decisions, One Big Victory for Civil Rights," *Trial*, September 2004.

Ronald Dworkin, "What the Court Really Said," *New York Review of Books*, August 12, 2004.

Jenny S. Martinez and David D. Caron, "Availability of U.S. Courts to Review Decision to Hold U.S. Citizens as Enemy Combatants—Executive Power in the War on Terror," *American Journal of International Law*, October 2004.

David B. Rivkin Jr. and Lee A. Casey, "Bush's Good Day in Court," *Washington Post*, August 4, 2004.

Philip Shenon, "U.S. Signals End to Legal Fight over an 'Enemy Combatant,'" *New York Times*, August 13, 2004.

Scott Turow, "Scalia the Civil Libertarian?" *New York Times Magazine*, November 26, 2006.

Mike Whitney, "Forcing Exile; Revoking Citizenship: The Real Meaning of the *Hamdi* Case," *CounterPunch Online*, October 13, 2004. www.countepunch.org.

Benjamin Wittes, "Enemy Americans," *Atlantic Monthly*, July/August 2004.

Hamdan v. Rumsfeld

Corine Hegland, "Foggy Crystal Ball for Detainees," *National Journal*, July 8, 2006.

Michael Isikoff, Stuart Taylor Jr., and Daniel Klaidman, "The Gitmo Fallout," *Newsweek*, July 17, 2007.

Adam Liptak, "The Court Enters the War, Loudly," *New York Times*, July 2, 2006.

Jonathan Mahler, "A Check Against Fear," *New York Times Magazine*, July 9, 2006.

Peter J. Spiro, "*Hamdan v. Rumsfeld*," *American Journal of International Law*, October 2006.

Supreme Court Debates, "Military Tribunals and the Court," September 2006.

James Taranto, "Ignorance of the Law," *American Spectator*, July/August 2007.

Nathan Thomburgh et al., "Gitmo. How to Fix It," *Time*, July 10, 2006.

Wall Street Journal, "Terrorists and the Supreme Court," April 1, 2006.

John Yoo, "Congress to Courts: 'Get Out of the War on Terror,'" *Wall Street Journal*, October 19, 2006.

Boumediene v. Bush and *Al Odah v. The United States*

Atlantic Monthly, "Guantanamo's Shadow," October 2007.

Joseph Blocher, "Combatant Status Review Tribunals: Flawed Answers to the Wrong Question," *Yale Law Journal*, December 2006.

Marjorie Cohn, "Why *Boumediene* Was Wrongly Decided," *Jurist*, February 27, 2007. http://jurist.law.pitt.edu.

William Glaberson, "U.S. Mulls New Status Hearing for Guantanamo Inmates," *New York Times*, October 15, 2007.

William Glaberson and Margot Williams, "Military Insider Becomes Critic of Hearings at Guantanamo," *New York Times*, July 23, 2007.

New York Times, "Gitmo: A National Disgrace," June 6, 2007.

Clive Stafford Smith, "From Guantanamo to Worse," *New Statesman*, July 16, 2007.

Wall Street Journal, "Terrorist Due Process," June 7, 2007.

Index